DRIVING AMBITIONS
Copyright © 1993 by Lauren Jonas Fix

Published by CALIFORNIA MUSTANG SALES AND PARTS, INC.

All rights reserved.
Reproduction of any portion of this book in any form,
for any reason, is strictly prohibited.

Editing and design by Janine Perkins
Illustrations by Teri Hiroko Osato

ISBN 0-9624908-7-3

Library of Congress Catalog Card Number 93-72931

Printed and bound in the United States of America.

DRIVING AMBITIONS

A Complete Guide to Amateur Auto Racing

LAUREN JONAS FIX

FOREWORD

In America, the automobile is universal. It affects everyone's life and, for many people, it defines more than simple transportation. Cars become hobbies, then those hobbies progress to becoming intense pursuits. "First time" experiences are universal--*everyone* is a beginner at some time or another.

Getting a car to accelerate is a problem of power versus inertia. Getting a human to overcome the inertia of inactivity, whether due to lack of confidence, shyness, or priorities, takes the power of knowledge. Sometimes it is difficult not to be intimidated by the mechanical aspects, the sheer torque, or the complicated operations of some cars. Also, it is hard on the ego to admit lack of knowledge. No one wants to go to a racing venue or a show site and be "the dumb one."

Any prospective enthusiast must accept this truth on faith: it is one hundred times better to admit a lack of knowledge than to falsely try to come across as a near-expert. The real experts will appreciate your honesty and will respond to your curiosity. Trying to come off as a know-it-all could turn off someone who might have been helpful.

Another problem remains: experts don't always have time to deal with novices. The beginner must find ways to acquire a fundamental knowledge before entering the ring. There are too few sources of information for enthusiasts who choose to pursue regional competition. It is difficult to learn the basics of involvement. Hence, this book.

Lauren Jonas Fix began her learning process more than 15 years ago. A woman in a man's world, Lauren not only had to endure her first years of learning the rules and methods, the toughness and the etiquette, the joys and foibles of competitive driving and concours shows, but also had to prove herself as a person. While more women are involved at all levels of today's competition, the lessons Lauren mastered under difficult circumstances remain as hurdles to be crossed by all newcomers to the sport.

In this book, in plain language, Lauren outlines the various requirements and steps which prospective drivers, team managers, or weekend enthusiasts must recognize. With her own experiences plus advice from accomplished colleagues, Lauren softens many of the intimidating factors for rookies and prepares drivers at all levels for the realities of the amateur racing world. She helps beginners steer away from typical beginners' problems in the car show realm.

Put simply, this book makes it clear that anyone, male or female, can achieve respect, success, and fun in automotive activities. Once an individual sets goals, learns the equipment, masters being patient and deliberate, learns when to be tough and when not to be tough, and learns his or her strengths and weaknesses, the rest is the fun part.

That's the main point. Make it fun.

Tom Corcoran
Editor, *Mustang Monthly*

ACKNOWLEDGMENTS

I am sincerely grateful to my father, H. George Jonas, for always supporting me through the years when I had doubts and my hopes had faded.

Additional thanks to my husband, Paul D. Fix II, for guiding me through this book and giving his advice and support through the whole project.

My sincere thanks also goes to Tom Corcoran, who started me on this project and helped nurture my ideas into final copy. When I was unsure, he helped me find some solid ground to continue.

The research material from the Sports Car Club of America was of great assistance to the project. They were extremely helpful every time we needed anything.

I truly appreciate the time, patience and friendship of Joseph Stallone in helping me to get the photos together for this book.

So many others have helped in countless ways that it is impossible to name them all, but I sincerely appreciate the effort of each one.

Photo Credits:
Cover
Gordon L. Jolley Motorsports Photography,
Grassroots Motorsports magazine, Conley Performance Plus
Chapter 1
Lancaster National Dragway, Lancaster, NY,
Joseph Stallone Photography
Chapters 3, 5
Joseph Stallone Photography
Chapter 4
Fast Track High Performance Driving School, Charlotte, NC,
Joseph Stallone Photography

CONTENTS

Chapter 1
Drag Racing 1

Chapter 2
Road Rallies 25

Chapter 3
Autocross 47

Chapter 4
Driving Schools 73

Chapter 5
Car Shows 105

Chapter 6
Before You Panic 121

Appendix
Clubs and Organizations 123

Log Book 134

Definitions for italicized words are located at the end of each chapter in the chapter glossary.

CHAPTER 1

Drag Racing
A Beginner's Guide To Bracket Racing

Drag racing tends to be something we think about at traffic lights, with one eye on the car in the next lane, the other eye watching for the police. It never fails that when you are driving the slowest car you own, some kid in a hot car wants to race. Naturally, no one will challenge you when you're driving your faster car.

Such is life.

Of course, street racing is not the safest way to compete. There are too many obstacles to avoid. Street traffic and keepers of the speed are major considerations. Police officers can ring up points on your license and set you back plenty of money. Dodging obstacles such as pedestrians and other cars is just plain dumb. Street racing is just not very intelligent.

Legitimate competitors know that a safe race against an experienced driver, under even conditions, with solid machinery and a raft of strategies, is ten times more rewarding than screeching your way from one city intersection to the next.

Let's progress beyond the civic nuisance level, and learn how big boys and girls compete.

DRAG RACING

Bracket Basics

There are two basic kinds of organized *drag racing*: *heads-up racing* and *bracket racing*.

Heads-up racing, similar to street racing, involves two cars accelerating after the lights come down. It is not the best way to compete because every car is built and set up differently.

Bracket racing is more competitive than heads-up racing, because each car receives a handicap, similar to golf or bowling. The race is based on reaction time, talent, and automotive performance.

The bracket racer first establishes the car's ideal time, or *dial-in* time, in the *time trials*. The competition progresses to eliminations, where the car with the biggest handicap leaves the line slightly ahead of the other car. Each car tries to beat the other to the finish line without going faster than its dial-in time. Obviously, driver consistency plays a large part in success.

You don't have to own a professional drag car to bracket race. There is a class for every car. A stock Mustang, Camaro, or even a pickup truck can compete. Plus, it doesn't take a genius to understand the bracket racing and handicap system. Understanding the rules will earn you respect, make you competitive, and there might even be some money in it for you.

Most drag strips are quarter-mile tracks, though some are one-eighth or even one-sixteenth of a mile. Track length can be a result of limited space, local ordinances, and the original finances of the owners or builders.

Each track will have its own configuration, but there are certain standard elements to the layout. You need to familiarize yourself with important

DRAG RACING

areas such as the *technical inspection* area, the *staging lanes* (which may be restricted to certain classes), the *water box* for *burnouts*, the starting area, the *speed trap*, the *timing booth*, and the refueling area.

The Road To Success

Many people believe that drag racing is easy, that it's a one shot deal, and that anyone can drive in a straight line. If it were that simple, anyone could win a race his or her first time out. However, because bracket racing requires a combination of talent and knowledge, that first-time win is somewhat unlikely. Yet the road to victory can be traveled by anyone if they learn the basics first.

Success may not arrive overnight--be patient. The longer you stick around, the more you'll learn. Why pay an entry fee and be eliminated in the first round week after week?

Don't expect to show up at a track and ask others for help. They're busy prepping their own cars and will probably not have time to help you. To solve that rookie dilemma, this chapter will outline the basics of bracket racing and offer a few secrets to help you get your money's worth the first time out.

By the way, exotic advice from other drag racers can be helpful down the road, but get the fundamentals down first. Be leery of competitors in your class. They won't always have your best interests at heart. An experienced friend in another class, however, can make you feel part of the group.

Finally, be open-minded, but competitive. It's a great way to meet people.

DRAG RACING

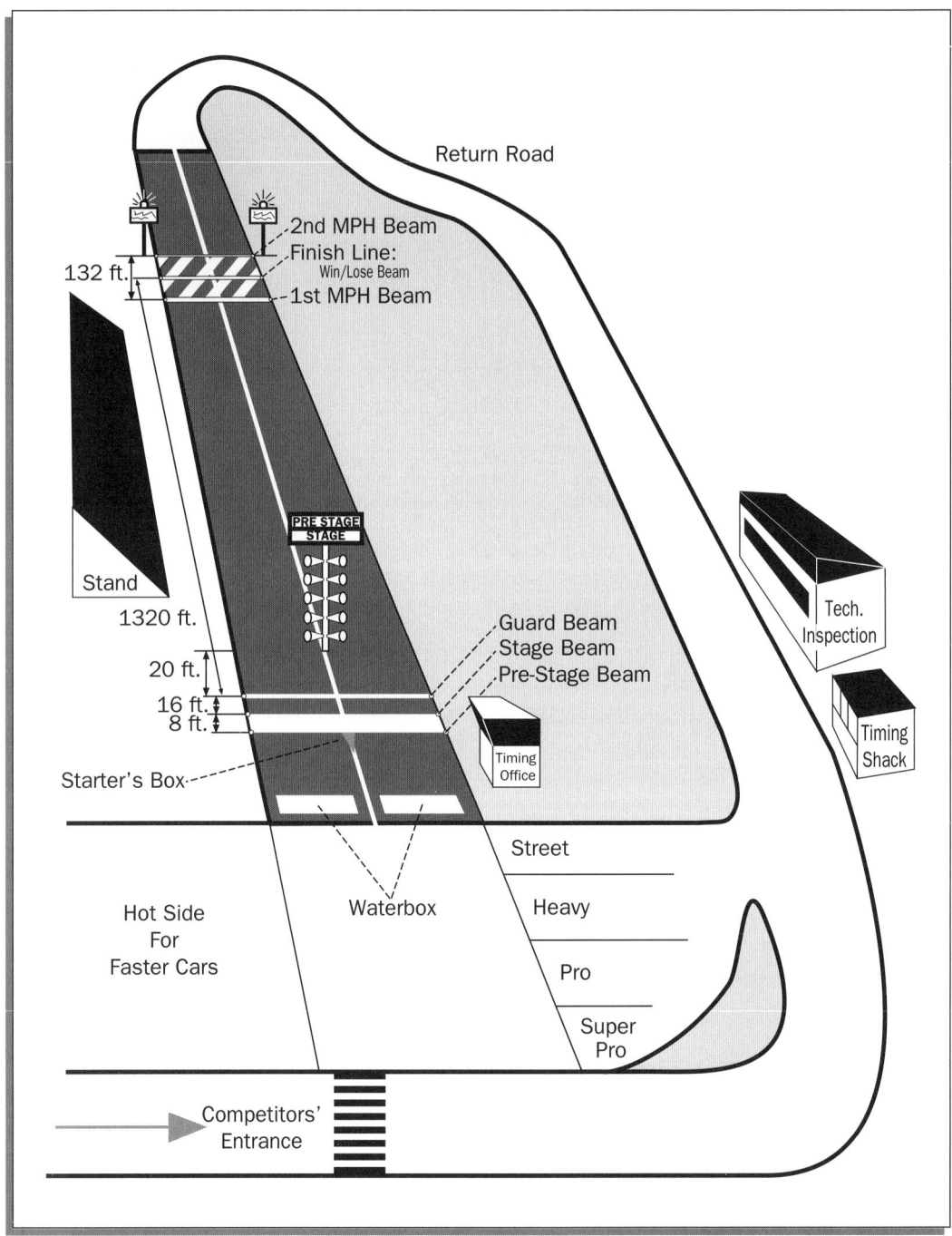

The drag strip

DRAG RACING

The Entry

As a participant, you will come through the competitor's entrance. At the credentials office, expect to pay about $20 per car and driver to enter the track. You may also be given the option of purchasing a license. This is not necessary unless you are running for year-end points. Check with your local track to be sure of *IHRA* or *NHRA* rules.

Before you leave the credentials office, ask for a schedule. Check to see when your first time trial starts. Then be sure to ask someone where to park during the event. It's extremely embarrassing to find yourself in the Top Fuel pits with a bone stock Ford Pinto.

The Inspection

As you make your way toward the track, get in line for the technical inspection.

Tech inspectors will require that there be no loose items in your car. Everything, including your floor mats and tools, will have to be removed before racing. Your seatbelts, steering, brakes, and seatbacks will be checked for function and safety in the interior. Be prepared to open your trunk, too. The spare tire and jack can remain if tied down properly, but nothing else should be left in the trunk.

The officials will also check your brake lights. Under the hood, they'll confirm that your battery is secure, and that there are no leaks or drips from the engine. A coolant overflow tank is required, even if it is a pop can or plastic bottle. No one wants to drive through anti-freeze and then try to get traction. Also expect the officials to check the carburetor return spring.

DRAG RACING

It's always best to cooperate rather than to hassle tech inspectors. Remember, they have teched hundreds of cars. It is not their fault if there is a problem with your car. Don't give them a tough time.

When you pass tech, the inspector will either give you a sticker, or will write your class and number on your car windshield. Many of these variables depend on the current year's competition rules set by NHRA, IHRA or whichever organization is sanctioning your race.

Leaving the inspection area, you'll probably be directed to get into one of a number of lanes behind several other drag racers. When it's your turn in line, you will be told to pull out of your lane by a track worker. Never pull out until directed to do so. Jumping into a race with another class without permission may give the track officials cause to ask you to leave.

The Track

Before your first time trial or elimination round, let's walk through all the stages of a typical run, from burnout to finish line.

The Burnout

The track will have a burnout area 30 to 40 feet behind the starting line. This concrete water box is topped with a thin layer of water. Always drive around it, then back up into the box. Water on your front tires won't help traction.

The idea is to place the rear wheels on the patch and accelerate off quickly without crossing the starting line. If you have a line lock (a special aftermarket item that allows you to lock only the front brakes while the rear wheels are free to spin), continue to warm your tires until a little smoke starts. This will be enough until you get the driving part down.

Don't start your burnout until the starter or track worker signals you to. Usually, they'll wait until the cars in front of you have left the starting line. Watch the other racers' techniques for pointers on the burnout area.

Depending on the track, a burnout may not be allowed at all if you don't have slicks. Burnouts are not recommended for street tires--all it does is wear out the tread and chunk up the tires. Most street tires on slower cars, such as pickup trucks, don't need to use the burnout area anyway. It's simply not going to help the traction. Remember that, with slicks, you'll probably be scraping rubber off your quarter panels the next day.

The Tree

At some early point in your learning curve, you should walk to the end of the staging lane to look at the Christmas tree--also called the *tree*. The tree displays two vertical rows of lights, one row for each lane. The top two lights are the *pre-stage* and *stage* lights. They are followed by three count down lights, to the green light. The red light at the bottom signals a false start.

The lights are triggered by photo-cells--beams of light across the starting line, near ground level. One set of photocells is located between the lanes on the starting line, with matching lights outside the lanes.

Staging Lights. As you pull up to the starting line, your front tire will break the pre-stage beam. That will illuminate the top bulbs. At this point I pause--once the next set of bulbs lights on both sides, the race begins.

The timing tree, or Christmas tree, from the top: prestage lights, stage lights, 3 amber lights, 1 green light, 1 red light.

DRAG RACING

Now, roll exactly eight inches farther, and your front tire will break the stage beam to illuminate the second set of bulbs on your side of the tree. The car next to you will do this at the same time.

Some systems have a third beam of light, called the guard beam, located 16 inches beyond the stage beam. In this case, the clock starts when the guard beam is crossed. The guard beam was designed to accommodate *rails, or* Top Fuelers; Pro Stock drag cars; and Funny Cars. Their low bodywork blocks the stage beam long after leaving the line, delaying the start of the clock until the car is a few feet away from the starting line. The added guard beam eliminates inherent timing flaws the dual-beam system creates.

Only eight inches separate the prestage and the stage ground beams.

Now your car is staged. One last option is *deep staging*, an advanced maneuver not recommended for first-timers. In deep staging, the car moves a little closer to the starting line by clearing the pre-staging beam, causing the top set of bulbs to go out.

Deep staging is usually unnecessary, so if you decide to try it, be aware that most tracks require that "DEEP" be printed on your windshield with shoe polish or letters.

Below the staging lights are three to five larger amber lights, then one green light and one red light. Currently, the five amber light tree is being phased out in favor of the three-light style.

The time spacing between the amber lights can be 0.25-second to as long as 0.50-second, though

DRAG RACING

the difference is not particularly critical because you'll get the feeling by counting "one - two - three" in your head.

Nodding slightly will help you get the rhythm of the lights.

The idea is to position your car on the line so you can accelerate when the last amber comes on without illuminating the bottom red bulb (sometimes called the "red eye"). To *red light* is to leave the starting line and cross the starting beams too early, before the green light comes on.

Handicap Lights. You may also notice two little amber lights at the bottom of the tree. They indicate that a handicap has been figured into the light sequence. A handicapped start allows for a perfectly-matched race at the finish line. This will occur only during eliminations, after completion of the time trials and dial-ins.

The Finish Line

Your speed will be measured at two different points and averaged: 66 feet in front of the actual finish line, and 66 feet after the finish line. The speed trap for quarter-mile tracks is 132 feet long, and is adjusted for other track lengths proportionately. If you back off the throttle at the finish line, your speed readout will not be accurate.

The Time Trial

Now that you've got the basics, let's run through a typical day at the races, starting with your time trial.

A time trial gives you a chance to show what your car can do, but lighting up your tires to make a scene is not what it's all about.

A time trial is not a race, so don't think about winning. Because cars of different classes can be matched during time trials, it's not over if you

What To Bring To The Races

Required:
1. Helmet, DOT or Snell 85 or better
2. White shoe polish for lettering and dial-in times
3. Glass cleaner and towels to remove or change shoe polish
4. Tire pressure gauge
5. Notebook -- and don't forget a pen
6. Basic tools in case you have a break down
7. Money, at least $20 to cover entry fees, food, etc.

Optional:
Plan ahead, remembering that you'll have to unload your car before you can race, so you'll need a place to put everything.

- A tire pump and/or air tank
- An extra set of spark plugs, at least one more heat range cooler than you run on the street, and a backup set of standard street plugs
- A plug wrench and socket
- Jets, bowl gaskets, and power valves
- A distributor wrench
- A timing light
- Thickness gauges
- A spare points set, condenser, point file, and contact cleaner
- Jumper cables
- Fender covers and rags
- A jack and jack stands
- Racers tape (duct tape)
- Tie wraps (nylon ties)
- A few spare header bolts
- Oil, at least one quart
- Automatic transmission fluid

Remember, the time for major changes is NOT at the track or between rounds. You should make sure the car is together and prepped before going to the track. The track is not a good place to test new bolt-on parts.

DRAG RACING

lose. You could even have a time trial against a top fuel car, although this is unlikely.

Usually, you can get two or more time trials, depending on the type of meet. You'll need at least two time trials to get an idea of what you and your car are capable of attaining.

Pay attention to everything you do--this is a time to form good drag racing habits. Because consistency is the basic idea behind bracket racing, you'll want to repeat the good habits over and over. In the early stages of your drag racing career, you want to learn, but you'll also want to win.

Once you're off the line and approaching the finish line, there are some things to keep in mind. After you break the speed trap, slow down safely and enter the return road. Be aware of your competitor's location. Many accidents happen when two drivers rush to go down the return road first. This is not part of the race, and both competitors receive the same information. So be sure to use your mirrors.

The timing system is located in the timing tower. The super system shown here is fully computerized to figure handicaps, reaction times, elapsed times, trap speed, short times and results.

As you proceed down the return road and cool down your vehicle, you may see cars from the *hot side* dumping water and hooking up their cars. Do not stop to help. They have their own pit crews and support teams, and you'll only be holding up traffic on the return road.

Stop at the timing shack and pick up your time slip. Head back to the pits, read the results of your run, and compare them to previous runs.

Please note that it is impossible to guess what your quarter-mile time will be based on an

DRAG RACING

eighth-mile result, and vice versa, without a computer.

Carry a notebook with you to log any adjustments made between runs. This will tell you if things are getting better or worse with each modification. Good habits will help improve your skills and tuning quicker than most beginners.

The Time Slip

You may find a listing on your time slip called *short time*. This is the 60-foot reading--your elapsed time for the first 60 feet of the race. Compare your time slips. You'll see that runs with faster short times have better run times and better *reaction times*.

The time slip will also show your car number, dial-in time, reaction time, trap speed, elapsed time, and results (win or lose). It will list the same information for your competitor. It's a good idea to keep your old time slips and date them. They will help you improve and see how different changes affect your time.

```
       LANCASTER     DRAGWAY
     BROADELM  GENERALS  GO

       1971 - - CAR NUMBER - -    302
      10.89 - -   DIAL-IN   - -  12.10
      11.233 - ELAPSED   TIME - 12.227
      66.27 - - TRAP SPEED - -   56.32
       .549 - REACTION  TIME -    .664
       2.886 - - SHORT TIME - -  2.712
              - - - RESULT -(*)-   WIN
```

Sample time slip

The rest is up to you. Keep your car tuned properly and, at each event, line up for as many time trials as possible. That alone will help you decide the pace you can run at consistently. Consistency is key to winning.

Eliminations: Dialing In And Breaking Out

Remember the purpose of time trials--they allow you to get a baseline of what your car is capable of running over a certain distance.

DRAG RACING

Eliminations are more involved, and this is the time to gamble. Now you will bet that you can run slightly slower or exactly on, but not faster than, your dial-in time. Doing so will allow you to win each elimination round and the overall race.

Certain variables can cause your elapsed times to fluctuate tremendously. For example, on an eighth-mile track, a slower car might produce two time trials of 12.13 and 11.99 seconds. The times are not that close, but it may be all you have to work with.

Now you know that the fastest your car goes is 11.99 (though it should get faster with experience). Which time should you dial in? Consider the length of time between elimination runs, whether this is a day or evening event, and the general air temperature. Each variable can affect your times as the event continues.

An evening event will help your car go faster as the air gets cooler. A day event progresses in the opposite direction, because engines are less efficient in warm air, and the engine doesn't cool as quickly. If there is a long time period between elimination runs, your car may become totally cold. This isn't good either--you'll end up warming your engine while in line for eliminations.

My first time at the track, a friend introduced me to an experienced drag racer named Skinny. He taught me all the tricks to dialing in, and sometimes we still discuss my times, because you can never guess exactly every time.

Because I usually run evening events, I know that I would choose the quicker dial-in time of 11.99. Your choice should be based on what you think you can run consistently.

Write your chosen time on the windshield next to the class and car number already written by

DRAG RACING

tech inspection. You may be allowed to change the number after each elimination, depending on the class. With experience, you'll have a general idea of what your dial-in will be for the next event.

Use white shoe polish to write on your windows. It comes off with glass cleaner and a rag.

During eliminations, the slower car will always start first. The time between competitors' starts--the interval between the light sequences--is the handicap.

You should be aware of your competitor's dial-in so that you'll know whether you will leave the line first, or wait a fraction of a second more. Don't be surprised if your light runs completely through the tree and the other guy waits a second or two. The times can be that far apart.

If you run faster than the time on your windshield, you *break out*. This means you will lose, unless the person you are racing breaks out also, and to a greater degree. For example, if you break out by running under your dial-in time by one-tenth of a second, and your competitor breaks out by two-tenths, you'll win because you are closer to your dial-in.

Techniques And Strategies

Keep in mind three truths about drag racing:
- *The quarter mile* is shorter than you think. It disappears quickly, even in a slow car.
- *The car's reaction time* is an extremely important variable. You will learn that 95 percent of a race is won or lost on the line.
- *If your car is staged properly*, the rest will fall into place.

Off The Line

What we call *cutting a good light* is the most important part of drag racing. The old adage, "If you snooze, you lose," is the most accurate

14

DRAG RACING

expression you'll ever hear in drag racing. Cutting a good light means leaving the starting line at the right time.

Human reaction time, from the time the eye sees the light to the time the foot reacts, is approximately 0.17-second. In racing, reaction time is recorded from the time the green light goes on until the time the staging beams are fully cleared.

A successful starting line technique requires that you leave on the last yellow before the green light. Your predetermined reaction time allows for the car to launch without getting the red eye. Remember, the green light illuminates only 0.50-second after the last yellow light comes on.

Deducting your reaction time from this half second leaves 0.33-second for a zero-reaction time. Seasoned racers have reaction times of 0.51-second or less, meaning their front tires clear the beam within 0.10-second of the green light. A perfect reaction time is 0.50-second.

Don't expect to get a perfect reaction for a while. Trying too hard to get a perfect reaction will cause you to red eye. This could be painful if you're into the money round. NHRA rules state that even if your opponent breaks out after you red light, you still lose because you blew it first.

Try to pad your reaction time a little, because a 0.55-second reaction time is respectable. The secret is to be consistent all the time in your anticipation and timing. But don't wait too long. If you wait for the green light to illuminate before you leave the starting line, you'll have a one-second, or worse, reaction time. And that may drop you from the first round of eliminations.

"One out of the money" is a sad, common story of drag racers who are eliminated just before the money round because they try to cut a better light.

DRAG RACING

Ten Drag Don'ts

Try to avoid making these mistakes:
1. Drive through the water box.
2. Smile for photographers or listen to the announcer when you are on the starting line.
3. Watch your competitor stage.
4. Watch your competitor's light come down.
5. Red light at the start.
6. Wait for the green light.
7. Cross the line in the middle of the track.
8. Cross the outer white lines.
9. Break out from your dial-in time.
10. Forget that weather can effect your times.

This all may seem like an impossible task, but it's a function of the car's position, your hours of practice, and sheer driving skill. With the proper conditioning, you only need nerves of steel and unwavering consistency in the face of extreme mental pressure to get great reaction times without red lighting.

There are many race strategies, but remember the basics: if your dial-in time is correct, and your opponent's is correct, the winner will be determined by inches and reaction times. You need to develop a technique for clocking near-zero reaction times at the starting line. A lot of little tricks can be picked up from fellow drag racers.

Rollout

Rollout is one factor that can give you that consistent improvement in reaction time. Rollout is the distance your car will roll from its starting position at rest until the clock starts.

Regardless of how quickly your car reacts, you

DRAG RACING

will need to use a little rollout to your advantage.

A great way to work with rollout is to pull up to the line until the pre-stage light comes on, then stop, and roll slowly until the stage light comes on, bumping the car up on the line just a bit. This brings you closer to the guard beam. If you pull up too far, you'll shut off the pre-stage light and go into deep staging.

I race a 1980 Ford Fiesta and have to bump in only a little beyond the staging light. Any more and there's a red light waiting for me.

Rollout is something you have to play with a little. The better you get, the less rollout you'll need until you reach that perfect spot to get excellent reaction times.

A note of caution: on some trees you will see two tiny yellow lights. This means that the light sequence will come down immediately the moment both you and your opponent stage. This may not leave enough time to stage slowly. If you hold up the race too long, some tracks will red light your lane for delay of race.

Reiterating, the pre-stage and stage beams are only eight inches apart, so there's not much rollout to work with. Each track may require you to adjust your rollout. Tire, engine, or chassis changes may also necessitate adjustments to your standard rollout.

Many tracks offer time-trial days. This is a great way to get your reaction times down, with no distractions from eliminations.

The idea is to have the car run as consis- tently as possible, so everything reacts the same way every time. Consistency is the most important thing, not speed. It is the only real key to winning at the *digs*.

DRAG RACING

Track Details

Track officials may use a deck of cards to insure fair lane assignments. The red card represents the right lane, and the black represents the left lane. A draw of two red cards means that two cars from the right lane race each other. One red and one black card indicate that a car from each lane will race. This method makes it virtually impossible to know who you will race.

A *bye run* is the way the rules balance out an uneven number of cars. In a field of 31 cars, there will be 15 races. The odd car will run down the track without a competitor and advance to the next round automatically.

The bye run may also be chosen with cards. A red five means the car in the right lane, five cars back, will get the bye run. That car will be held up until all the cars in the class have run. It will then get the bye run.

Over the long haul, everyone lucks into a few bye runs; one is allowed per race event. You can't lose, red light, or break out in a bye run. It's an instant win. Some tracks will time them. On others, you'll just drive to the end. You must, however, drive your car down the track.

If it should rain before or during time trials, the track may offer a rain date ticket to each competitor. The date won't be at your convenience; it will most likely be a free pass to the next event only. If it rains during eliminations, two things could happen. It may mean the end of the event, or a track official might write down each competitor's name, dial-in time, and car number for a rain date elimination. All rain date information will be given by the track if it rains.

DRAG RACING

Money Rounds

As you improve, you'll find yourself making it to the finals, or the money rounds. If there were 20 cars to start, after the first eliminations there will be 10 cars, and the second round will have five cars. Most tracks pay out four places, so this means three cars compete for money after the third elimination round. One car gets the bye run.

The two cars that won and the bye run car compete for first-, second-, and third-place money. The two losers of the third elimination run for fourth-place money.

Here's a secret I learned the tough way: don't remind your opponent of the next race. If he doesn't show, you automatically win fourth-place money. A bye run for fourth place is better than racing and being one out of the money.

Don't feel guilty. Your opponent probably wouldn't tell you either. A friend once ran the bye run for $25 and I went home empty handed. I never knew what happened until it was all over but, fortunately, he was nice enough to tell me so it wouldn't happen again.

The Inside Stuff

It's time to consider some things you should know and probably will never read or hear about, unless a friend tells you or you witness an experienced competitor in action. These advanced strategies are to be used only after you have learned how to consistently cut a good light. Strategy won't do you any good if you can't get beyond the first round.

The "psyche-out" has some great advantages when there are large numbers of cars, or a more experienced driver is your opponent. It's a mind

DRAG RACING

game, but you can win with the right attitude.

Don't walk in thinking you're hot stuff and no one can touch you. It's a poor way to make friends, and it can give you a bad reputation from the start. The one who is cool and keeps his secrets to himself is the one who will succeed. Just like playing cards, you'll notice most of your competitors will have poker faces.

Showing up at the drags in a fire suit for running in the street class is not a way to psyche others out. If you're a woman, heels, low-cut shirts, and high-cut shorts won't help you do anything except get hit on. Just like a poker face, you want to blend in. This should all be part of your psychological strategy.

Once you've completed your time trials, don't put your dial-in time on the window until just a few minutes before they call your class. This gives you time to check for changes in weather and also robs your competitors of the chance to see your dial-in until the last minute. If they are really interested, they can wait.

If you're not that successful at the drags, most opponents won't care or understand why you don't put your dial-in time on immediately. It's still a good habit, because the better you get, the more important it is to keep the times as unpublished as possible.

Keeping your time slips out of sight will also keep everyone guessing. I usually put mine in my ashtray or glovebox so I can review them.

If you can't change your times between rounds, don't cover up your dial-in after the first elimination. You've proven yourself if you can go beyond the first round. It's no longer a secret.

Another thing most opponents don't like is *sand bagging*. This is my personal favorite

DRAG RACING

because no one knows how fast the car really is.

The strategy is to write down a slower dial-in number so that you have the advantage. This can backfire if your opponent plays the same game, or if you're not good at it.

Say your car does 13.60 in the quarter mile, so you dial in 13.99. You will have less of a handicap, allowing you to get ahead and hit the brakes before the finishing line. You slow the car enough to avoid breaking out, but you cross the line first and win the race.

Another competitive edge is to allow your opponent to stage first, letting you collect your thoughts. Don't delay too long, though, or you'll red light. Watch other racers and you will see many competitors do this little psyche-out trick. It works, sometimes.

Drag racing can be done with any street vehicle. Note that the car on the left is deep staged.

DRAG RACING GLOSSARY

Italicized words found in this chapter:

Bracket racing. A race between two cars to determine which can accelerate faster, where a handicap is figured so that consistency is a greater factor than speed. Also known as ET (elapsed time) bracket racing.

Break out. When an elapsed time is faster than a dial-in time during eliminations.

Burnout area. Shallow concrete water trough located 30 to 40 feet behind the starting line, used for warming the rear tires. The driver accelerates out quickly, or uses a brake lock.

Bye run. Balances a field of an uneven number of cars. A single vehicle advances to the next elimination round without racing. One bye run is allowed per race.

Cutting a good light. Accelerating off the starting line to achieve a half-second or slower reaction time.

Deep staging. A technique that illumines only the staging light, moving a car closer to the starting line.

Dial-in time. The time you think you can run consistently. The object during eliminations is to run slower than your dial-in time.

Digs. Slang term for the drags or drag racing.

Drag racing. A fun automotive sport, including *heads-up* and *bracket racing*.

Heads-up racing. The original form of drag racing, with no handicapping. Determines which of two cars can accelerate the fastest from a standstill.

Hot side. Track separation of street vehicles from faster drag cars. Top Fuel, Funny Cars, Super Gas/Comp., and Pro Stock are hot side drag cars.

IHRA. International Hot Rod Association.

NHRA. National Hot Rod Association.

Pre-stage. To move your car into a position that triggers the first row of lights on the *tree*. The pre-stage bulbs are not lit when deep staging.

Rails. Drag cars using an open chassis made of long tubes, with either a front or rear engine. Top Fuel cars are rails.

Reaction time. The time it takes to cross the guard beam from the staging line (16 feet). A perfect reaction time is 0.50-second. Reaction time is based on hand/eye coordination.

Red light. Also known as a "red-eye"; breaking the guard beam in less than 0.50-second, or going before the light is green.

Rollout. The distance the car rolls from its starting position at the stage light, until the clock starts.

Sand bagging. Using a slower dial-in than the car can go, and braking at the finish line.

Short time. A measurement of time based on a 60-foot distance reading.

Speed trap. Top speed area, measured 66 feet before and after the finish line.

Staging. Once the second amber light is lit, your car is staged.

Staging lanes. The lanes adjacent to the racing area separating cars into their appropriate classes.

Technical (or tech) inspection. A necessary safety check by track officials performed before any car can race.

Time trial. A run down the track to get a baseline for your dial-in time. Two are usually allowed per event.

Timing booth. The place to pick up your time slip after the race at the end of the return road.

Tree. Also known as the Christmas tree. The column of lights including the prestage and stage lights, amber lights, green light and the red light.

Water box. See *burnout area*.

CHAPTER 2

Road Rallies
Instructions, Signs And Clues

In a *road rally* event, a driver/navigator team travels a specifically designated (and unfamiliar) route, while attempting to maintain varying average speeds assigned by the rally organizers.

Each car leaves the starting point at a precise time, and is expected to cross the finish at a mathematically-computed, ideal time.

Any type of motor vehicle may be used--this motorsport can be enjoyed in anything from a sportscar to a four-wheel drive pickup truck.

Rallies are run on public roads using all types of surfaces, including paved, gravel, and dirt. They usually start at automobile dealerships, shopping center parking lots, or restaurants. Rallies are generally held as scheduled, regardless of wind, rain, or snow. Only the most severe conditions--such as outright road closings--will postpone a rally.

Cooperation between driver and navigator is key to a successful rally. The driver's job is to maintain the specified average speed, while the navigator's job is to make computations and plans to keep the car on time and on the correct route.

Both participants must also be alert to find the proper route and to spot any directional clues. The two jobs really overlap, and the idea is to

ROAD RALLIES

work together to get through the maze as successfully as possible.

This basic description may sound easy, but *route instructions* are not generally as simple as "Turn left on Main Street." Instructions usually consist of tulip maps, string maps, written or mathematics problems, mileage notations, and obscure clues. That is all you get, plus a map to indicate the road rally boundaries.

Finding A Rally

You may hear of a rally from a friend, a poster in a parts store, or you may even receive a flyer in the mail. If you're interested but haven't seen or heard anything about rallies, contact your local *SCCA* office. They'll put you in contact with your local *rallymaster* or other rally groups.

Once you enter a rally, your name will get on a mailing list so you'll be aware of other rallies.

Rallying is a fun sport that has its own rules and vocabulary. This chapter provides a set of general instructions, a glossary of terms, and sample route instructions. Become familiar with all of them before attending your first rally.

Teamwork

Good teams have learned not to take anything too personally, and not to crumble at a single mistake. Many of the most successful rally teams are manned by husband/wife duos who have rallied together a great deal. Of course, combinations of family members or close friends do not always work to a team's advantage.

In my case, pairing an "A-type" personality at the wheel with an "A-type" navigator didn't work. We did so well, the winning went to our heads.

As we attended more rallies, we advanced to

> ### Rally Checklist
>
> Once you've convinced your spouse or intended rally partner that this will be fun (they'll have beer and a party at the end of the rally), collect all the items you'll require:
>
> 1. **A full tank of gas** in a car that is safe to take on a trip of approximately 100 miles
> 2. **Two clipboards**, or one board with two clips at the top: one for general instructions and blank paper, and the other for route instructions. For a custom rally clipboard, pop-rivet two clips at the top of a Plexiglas board and tape the CAS chart to it.
> 3. **Scratch paper** (plenty of it)
> 4. **Pencils and assorted colored markers**
> 5. **A calculator** with good batteries
> 6. **An accurate watch** with a second hand or digital display
> 7. **Maps** of the counties and cities where you may travel -- these are usually supplied by organizers
> 8. **A hand-held spotlight** and a light for writing during night rallies (a flashlight is inconvenient to write by)
> 9. **A CAS chart** -- Use the one supplied later in this chapter.

the more difficult route maps. We also fought constantly. One time my stubborn navigator got so mad that he chose to walk 20 miles rather than ride home. Needless to say, that partnership suffered. Thank God it did not result in marriage.

That particular example doesn't mean that you can't work well with your friend, spouse, or other relative. If you and a potential teammate can have an intelligent, calm conversation to sort out and solve a problem, then that person is a good rally partner candidate. I have seen father/daughter teams do extremely well, so don't fail to consider your children or parents, especially if they are great with math.

ROAD RALLIES

OFFICIAL REGISTRATION FORM

Event _____ Date _____

Class Entered _____

Driver Name _____ Navigator Name _____

Address _____ Address _____

City/State _____ Zip _____ City/State _____ Zip _____

Telephone No. _____ Telephone No. _____
                                                    (Navigator)

Would you consider joining a motorsport club? (Driver) _____

Make of Car _____ Model _____ Year _____

Where did you receive information about this rally? _____

TECH INSPECTION

Driver License _____   Seat Belts _____
Registration _____   Frame _____
Proof of Insurance _____   Head Lights _____
Brakes _____   Turn Signals _____
Tires _____   Brake Lights _____
Wipers _____   Back Up Lights _____
Horn _____   Tail Lights _____

Rally registration form

ROAD RALLIES

Registration

Once you've decided on the rally that interests you, it is a wise idea to pre-register. Normally, pre-registration can save you money. It also helps the rallymaster to gauge the probable attendance in order to have enough materials available.

I like to pre-register to get an earlier *out time*, so if we get lost there are still other competitors to help us get back on track. (Of course, that doesn't mean they are on track either. At a Ferrari Club road rally, about eight cars got turned around and ended up following each other. We all lost.)

If you choose to wait until the rally day to register, arrive early enough to complete the necessary paperwork. If you are pre-registered, check in at the location registration table. After verifying your participation, they will give you a car number and an out time.

There is usually a *drivers meeting* before a rally. Take notes on anything unusual. You will also receive a set of general instructions for the event and any maps or pertinent information.

Once this is done, be sure to synchronize your watch with the *official time*. This may be from *WWV*, the time signal broadcast nationwide by radio from the National Bureau of Standards, or from the rallymaster's watch. Accuracy to the second is important, because that one second could be the point that gives you first place.

Now that the preliminaries are finished, it's a good idea to mingle with the competitors and see how their cars are equipped. Don't be afraid to ask questions, but keep the subject to rallying. You'll learn something new every time.

ROAD RALLIES

Instructions And Clues

Sample instructions may be provided prior to an event. They will also be distributed to competitors at registration on the day of the event.

Review the sample instructions before the rally begins, to be sure that you understand them. The only way to execute all route instructions properly is to strictly follow the rules and procedures.

Actual route instructions will be given to you one minute before your out time. Read the first two directions, then the general instructions. Note anything important. The navigator should highlight speed changes and specially-defined words.

Use different colors to denote anything special. The more colors the better, within reason. Your style of marking is optional. Some people use drawings and notes to themselves.

General instructions give important details like when to ignore roads marked "dead end," "private," or "road closed." Where there are no instructions, go as straight ahead as possible, executing speed changes at the apex of turns or at the landmarks cited. Clues may also appear on either side of the road.

Don't be surprised if the general instructions sound like a riddle. A statement could be as unusual as, "All left turns take a right and vice-versa," or, "Skip all odd numbered instructions." There might even be puzzles. Distances may be cumulative or non-cumulative, and this will be stated in each section.

Checkpoints

Rally competitions are based on time, speed, and distance (*TSD*).

Along the assigned route are *checkpoints*, set up and manned by one or more rally organizers. These folks will note the exact time, to the second

ROAD RALLIES

or hundredths of a minute, that each car crosses a line at the checkpoint. The distance between checkpoints is varied, as are the speeds a contestant must average from point to point. Checkpoint locations are not known in advance to the car occupants. They may be just over a hill, around a curve, or visible at the next intersection.

Time lost due to traffic or improper navigation cannot be made up after a car is sighted by a checkpoint worker. A new *out time* will be given at each checkpoint. The score each car receives at each checkpoint is based upon how close it has come to the ideal time. The winner will have the fewest penalty points, and be closest to a perfect score.

This is a checkpoint. Remember to pass the check point and then bring your timing card back to the checkpoint timer.

Navigator Notes

While you might not mind being off course and speed (and time) too far on your first event, mileage-based turns may be critical. The navigator will probably give seat-of-the-pants directions for the first few rallies. Many events are actually won this way.

There can even be "checkpoints" that are off-course. If you see a checkpoint that is not on the route, do not enter it. It's a trick that will add to your point total. If the checkpoint is on the route, and the checkpoint sign is facing you, you must stop and check in or you'll receive penalty points for improper checkpoint procedures.

You will take clues from road configurations, mileages, written material, and objects observed along the road or route. The written material and

ROAD RALLIES

> *You won't get instruction like "Count the pairs of pink underwear on the clothesline at the Joneses' house." Who knows if the Joneses will keep their underwear out all day so that everyone can inspect it?*

objects may be signs, homes, barns, mailboxes, road surfaces, or other solid objects. You will only be given clues that can be observed while traveling at the instructed speeds; clues will not apply to moving or moveable objects, such as animals or people.

The Starting Line

The cars will line up in assigned numerical order. If the rally starts at noon, car number one will go at 12:01 p.m., car number two at 12:02 p.m., and so on.

Odometer Calibration

The odometer *calibration zone* section is always the first rally instruction. These basic directions are not meant to confuse you, but to compare your odometer with the rally master's odometer.

If you have changed your transmission, tire sizes, or rearend gears to anything other than the car's original specifications, you should expect to have an error in your odometer calibration.

You are allowed an exact amount of time for calibration. Any excess time is yours to read through the rest of the route instructions.

The Correction Factor

The mechanics of timekeeping start at the beginning of the rally.

Write down the actual odometer reading in miles, tenths of miles and, if possible, estimate hundredths of miles. The odometer check at the beginning of all rallies, usually about 10 miles long, is your first gauge of accuracy.

After completing the odometer check section, record the mileage reading on your car and

ROAD RALLIES

calculate the distance traveled as indicated on your odometer. If the distance is not equal to the mileage reference given as the *OD* check distance by the rallymaster, you will need to calculate a correction factor.

Your correction factor is equal to your mileage at the end of the OD check, divided by the official mileage of the OD check.

For example, the few instructions of a rally section may read:

- 8.75 Right at crossroads.
- 10.00 Straight on at junction right. Odometer check at "Schlemmer." CAS 40 mph. Take odometer reading.
- Pause 5 minutes anywhere within the next 1.00 mile to do calculations.
- 11.50 Straight on past junction left.
- End of section (EOS)
- Begin next section - zero your odometer.

If your car's odometer reading at the odometer check was 15328.85, and the odometer reading at the start of the rally was 15317.35, it shows the distance covered as 11.50. The actual distance was 10 miles, so your correction factor is 11.50 divided by 10.00, or 1.15.

To stay on time, you will need to multiply by this correction factor when calculating both speed and distance.

For example, if the specified speed is 30 mph, you would multiply 30 by 1.15 to find a corrected speed of 34.5 by your speedometer. If the instructions say to go 15 miles and turn right, you would multiply 15 by 1.15, then be sure to turn right only after 17.25 miles had passed on your odometer.

ROAD RALLIES

Technical Assistance

Aftermarket computers can be used by rallyists to calculate exact times and mileages. These expensive units do not guarantee a perfect score, but do help teams of varying experience. Use of such equipment automatically places your car in an advanced class. I recommend you stick with the basics at first. Later, you can request more information from the SCCA and fellow road rallyists to see what you will be getting into.

Now that you have completed your calibration zone, be sure to read any information about timing, controls (checkpoints), penalties and miscellaneous details. This is also a perfect time to read through each section, do calculations, and try to anticipate potential problems you may encounter during the rally.

Averaging Speeds

For most beginners, it is sufficient to have the driver do his or her best to maintain average speeds by proper acceleration and keeping an eye on the speedometer.

In order to win, however, you'll need to combine your knowledge and experience with speed and time tables and calculators to further improve your score.

Rally competitors who want to zero the checkpoints use a *CAS* (change of average speed) chart to adjust for stop signs, traffic, and traffic lights that may slow down a car's speed.

CAS Chart

If your car has the same OD reading as the rallymaster's, you can use this chart to accommodate for traffic delays.

If the CAS is :	Then travel at:
20 mph	22 mph
25 mph	28 mph
30 mph	33 mph
35 mph	39 mph
40 mph	44 mph
45 mph	50 mph
50 mph	55 mph

ROAD RALLIES

Use the CAS chart to make periodic increases above the average speed to compensate for obstacles. This technique will keep you in the ball park for low scores at the checkpoints.

Mileage

Mileage and turns may be cumulative or non-cumulative. Cumulative mileage instructions give the distance until the next turn or intersection starting from the beginning of the section. The end of each section is clearly marked *EOS*.

Non-cumulative instructions pinpoint turns from the execution of the previous instruction:

Cumulative mileage example:
0.00 Start of rally
1.50 Left at junction
1.75 Right at stop sign
2.63 Straight at intersection
4.80 Turn left at crossroads
End of section (EOS)

Non-cumulative mileage example:
0.00 Start of section (SOS)
1.43 Left
0.27 Right
0.95 Straight
2.26 Left

Maps

String Maps

String (strip) maps show a route traveled from point A to point B. String maps are not intended to be to scale, but it is possible that you may receive a scale for a section indicating something like "1 inch = 1 mile."

ROAD RALLIES

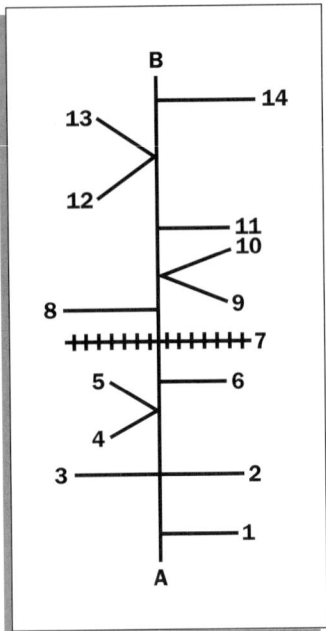

Your route instructions may look like this string map.

Look at a string map as if the route were stretched out into a straight line. Imagine that each line coming off the straight line tells you how many roads to leave on your left or right as you travel along the route of the section. All roads will be shown.

String map translation:
1. Leave a road to your right
2./ 3. Leave a road to the left and right
4. /5. Leave two roads to your left
6. Leave one road to your right
7. Cross railroad tracks
8. Leave one road to your left
9./10. Leave two roads to your right
11. Leave one road to your right
12./13. Leave two roads to your left
14. Leave one road to your right

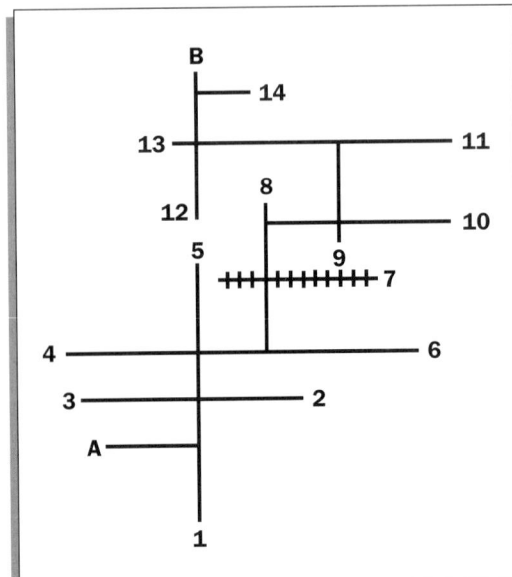

String map example (above) and the actual route map

Proceeding from point A to point B, you would come upon a "T" in the road (see the actual route map). You would note the string map's first instruction, telling you to leave road 1 on your right. In this case, you would turn left, and continue.

Should you come to an *intersection*, and the string map says to leave one road to your left and one road to your right, you would continue straight ahead.

As you may have observed, when following a string map you never know which way to turn

ROAD RALLIES

until you come to the next intersection.

Continue to go over the example until you understand this section. It can be tricky. Once you grasp the basics you will be amazed at how easy it is to understand.

Tulip Diagrams

A *tulip diagram*, an overhead view of an intersection, is a commonly-used route instruction. The position of the car before the intersection is indicated by the dot and the direction of travel is represented by the arrow.

The team is asked to carry out the instructions in numerical order. Of course, some rallymasters may tell you to use even or odd directions only.

My favorite is when the section instructions tell you to enter at the arrow and exit at the dot. As a rule, you always enter at the dot and exit at the arrow, unless otherwise stated.

Mileage may or may not accompany the diagrams. The tulips may also be placed in random order. The position of the dot may be on any

Typical tulip diagrams

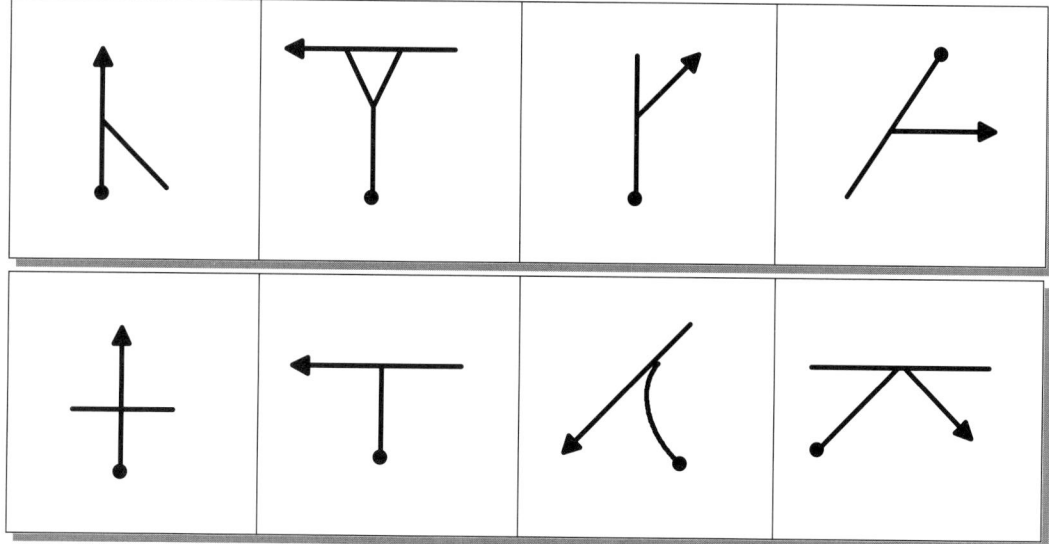

ROAD RALLIES

side of the box, so it may be necessary to rotate the instruction page to read the clue properly.

Finding Yourself

The rally or route instructions vary in degrees of difficulty. Some sections may be easier than others. It is not the intent of rallymasters to lose anyone so that they cannot complete the rally or enjoy it. If you do get lost within a section, there are several good approaches to take to get yourself back on route.

Try not to follow another competitor. Those people may be just as lost as you are, or they may be working on another section of the rally that uses the same road. Continue the section as stated. Everyone else will also be unsure--this is usually a little trick the rallymaster plays.

Many rallies use the same roads more than twice. If you see another competitor going the other way, it doesn't necessarily mean you are lost.

Some examples of tricks I've seen include sending cars one way down a road, then bringing them back a few instructions later, and using seasonal dirt roads or just part of an expressway to make drivers feel lost. There can even be checkpoints on each side of the road, so always follow your route.

If you get lost, do not try to execute the instructions from where you end up. Go back to where you knew you were on the route, review the directions carefully, and execute them again. Try to spot your earlier error, and avoid repeating the same mistake.

It is more important to stay on course than to be on time. However, do not spend an extended length of time trying to complete a section that will not work out for you.

The end of the section is stated within the

ROAD RALLIES

instructions for that section. Stop at an intersection. Locate yourself on a map provided, then drive to the end of the section you are on. Restart yourself there on the next section.

The section ends may be printed on the map provided at registration, or posted somewhere at registration. Make sure you copy down the section end locations. Even if you miss a checkpoint or two, you will be able to complete the rally.

If you do get back on track, the missed checkpoints will cost you points, but at least you learned something--and you finished the rally. The last checkpoint is usually just up the street from the finish location.

It is difficult to make up time spent recovering from miscalculations or missing the route. Don't assume anything. Be sure you read and understand the general instructions. Check off each route instruction as you complete it, but check it off only when it is completed. Checking off an item in advance is the surest way to miss that instruction altogether--you'll already be looking for the next one in line.

Most of all do not give up. If you are lost, or think you are, pull off the road and look things over calmly. Plan a recovery to get back on course by examining road maps and trying to recall significant landmarks. Don't take any shortcuts, and follow every instruction to the letter, even if the end is near. Do not read between the lines.

Emergency Instructions

You may have received an emergency envelope when you started. DO NOT open it--turn it in with your rally check point card. An open envelope will usually cost you 1000 points. Inside the envelope is a map giving the location of the finish, like a

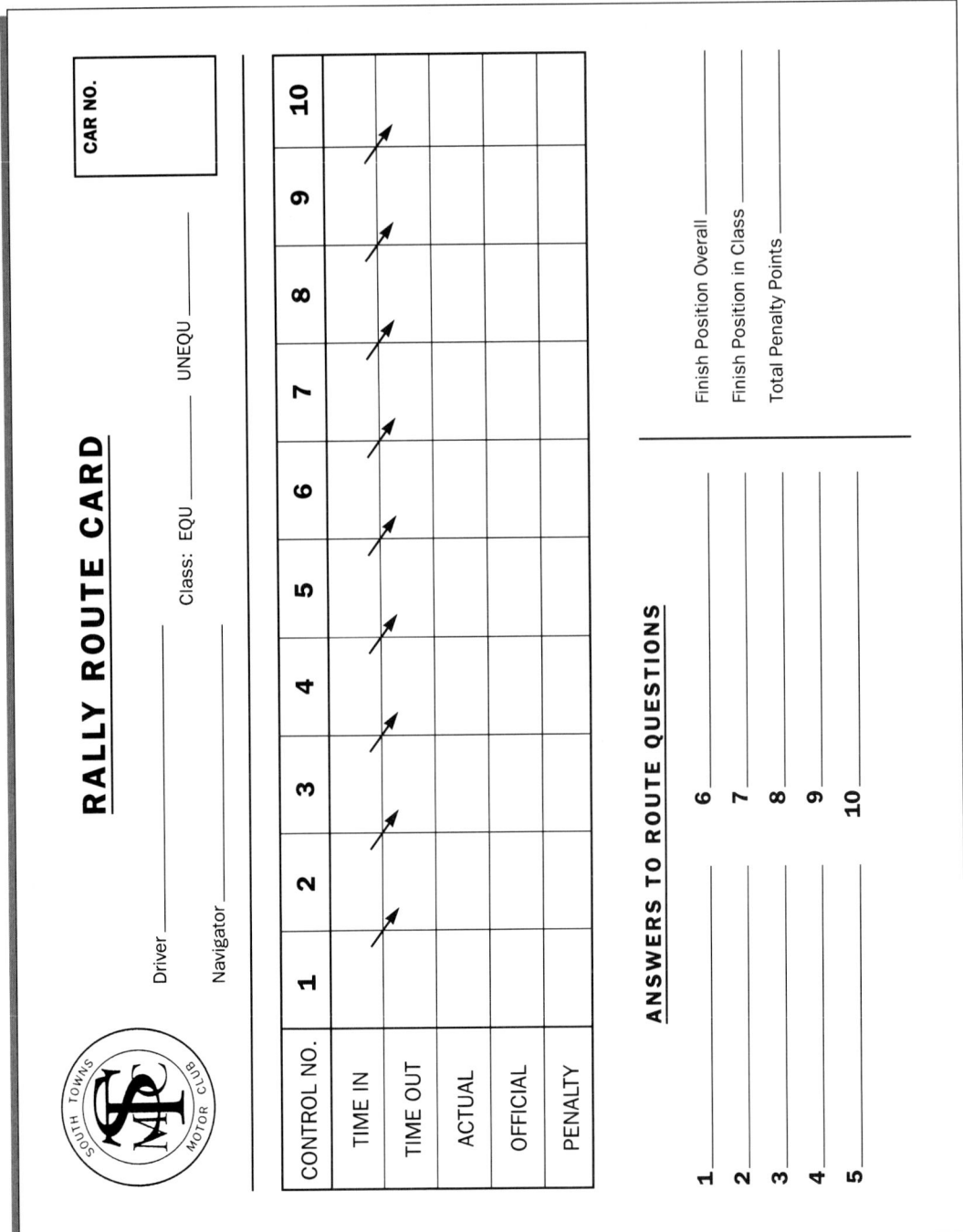

Rally route checkpoint card

ROAD RALLIES

bar or restaurant.

If you have totally given up hope of completing the rally, open the envelope and check in at the finishing location so the rallymaster doesn't think you have broken down or gotten totally lost. It is also a good time to talk to others to find out where you got lost, so the next time the same situation occurs you will be able to master that section.

Safety Concerns

A rally is not a license to speed or to drive recklessly. Most rallymasters will disqualify you if your team gets a ticket, so obey traffic laws and show courtesy to other drivers and participants. We once gave up a rally to help another competitor who drove too fast and totaled his brand new Saab. We stood by him until the wrecker came. The rallymaster dropped that section from the rally. Of course, the Saab owner got a *DNF* (did not finish).

Flat tires, running out of gas, or other misfortunes may ruin one section of a rally, but each section is scored separately.

Checkpoint workers usually stay an extra half-hour beyond the last car expected, just in case of a lost straggler.

Points And Scores

Scoring and penalty points are figured to the tenth of a minute. Your time is taken the instant the front of your car passes the checkpoint sign.

One penalty point is assessed for each .10 minute early or late at a checkpoint, unless the general instructions are stated otherwise.

Timing is non-cumulative. An early or late time one checkpoint cannot be accounted for at the next checkpoint. If you are running exactly on

ROAD RALLIES

time, you should enter the checkpoint at one of the odd multiples of five hundredths of a minute (.05, .15, .25, etc.). Checkpoints will record the time to the tenth of a minute by dropping the hundredths digit (.95 would be recorded as .9). This allows you to be approximately .05 minute early or late without penalty.

A checkpoint's out time will always be at the .00 mark of the minute assigned. Timing discrepancies should be noted by the checkpoint captain to be resolved at the finish. Once a competitor accepts their *in time*, it becomes official and cannot be changed.

Penalties

Penalties are usually assigned as follows:

1 point per tenth of a minute early or late at a checkpoint

200 points maximum time penalty at any checkpoint

200 points for checking in at an off-course checkpoint (with no penalty at the next checkpoint)

300 points for a missed checkpoint with no penalty at the next checkpoint.

500 points for improper checkpoint procedure, such as stopping within sight of a checkpoint area, unsafe entry into a checkpoint area, or entering a checkpoint from the wrong direction

1000 points for opening envelope supplied at start of rally

Disqualification can occur at the discretion of the rallymaster, for traffic or criminal violations, consumption of alcohol during the event, abusive language directed at the rallymaster or assistants, or for unsportsmanlike conduct.

The Finish

The rallymasters will figure the results at the end of the rally, after the last car has arrived. You will also receive a copy of the results in the mail. They will announce the results and award trophies.

When it is all over, ask any questions your team may have and get your name on a mailing list for future rallies. Travel the route of the rally over again to see where you lost points or detoured from the course. This is a good way to review your navigational skills and learn not to repeat errors.

Go ahead and try a rally. You may have to change partners, or you may also find you and your partner make a good team. It really is a fun sport and a great way to spend a Sunday.

Rallies are run all year 'round, and may be based on different themes such as Halloween costume runs, scavenger hunts and turkey runs. At a speed rally you can arrive early, but not late. We bring our fastest car, to get in as soon as possible.

Once you get the hang of rallying you might find yourself getting more involved with different clubs and organizations. Perhaps someday you'll even write your own rally!

ROAD RALLIES

Route Terms Directory

Definitions for common terms found in route instructions

Acute. A turn substantially more than 90 degrees.

After. The named navigational aid may be found anywhere along the rally route following execution of the immediately preceding route instruction.

At. The navigational aid will be visible along the rally route where a speed change or turn is executed.

Away from. A turn in the opposite direction of the indicated navigational aid visible from the intersection.

Bear. A turn substantially less than 90 degrees.

Before. The named navigational aid will be visible from the intersection of the instruction being executed.

Bridge. A structure over a river, railroad, or highway, to provide a way to cross.

Controls. Another name for checkpoints.

Cross. To go straight across. To cross a divided highway is to cross both halves of it.

Crossroads. An intersection in which two roads cross each other.

Delta. Another name for a triangle. Roads are on all three sides.

EOS. End of section

Follow. To stay on the named or numbered road until the next instruction. You will "follow" at least once before looking for the next clue.

Free zone. A specified section of the route containing no checkpoints.

Intersection. Any meeting or crossing of public roads.

Jog. A turn in one direction followed by a turn in the opposite direction within .20 mile. Execution always begins at the base of a "T" intersection. The jog can be onto a leg of the "T" or onto a crossroad.

Junction. An intersection in which two roads meet, but do not cross.

Pause. To delay a specified time. Add to or subtract your timing calculations at a given clue or before the next instruction.

Pickup. Go straight onto a new named, numbered route or type of road surface.

RRX. Where a set or sets of railroad tracks cross the road surface.

SAS. Start average speed.

SCCA. A sanctioning body for rallies.

SO. Straight on.

SOS. Start of section.

Tee. A point where one road terminates at another at a right angle, always approached from the bottom.

Transit Zone. A section of the route containing no check points. A specific time is given to travel the distance between two points. This time is included in the ideal time to reach the next check point.

Turn. A change of course or direction at an inter section.

Underpass. A bridge built to allow a roadway or railroad to go over the road.

Y. An intersection resembling the letter "Y," always approached from the bottom.

ROAD RALLY GLOSSARY

Italicized words found in this chapter:

CAS. Change of average speed. See CAS Chart for ten percent overages.

Calibration zone. A section mapped out by the rallymaster to compare actual distances to the rallymaster's odometer. You may have to use a correction factor to meet the exact distances.

Checkpoint. A checkpoint denotes the end of a section or a rally. It also can be found in the middle of a section. Times in and out are noted and used to compare to the perfect time, and to record penalties for all times off the perfect time.

DNF. Did not finish.

Drivers meeting. An important, mandatory meeting before every event.

EOS. End of section.

In time. The arrival time marked at a checkpoint.

Intersection. Any meeting or crossing of two or more public roads.

OD. Odometer

Official time. The official time is based on WWV short wave radio signals. The official time is the actual and correct time.

Out time. The time given to you by the checkpoint or starter at the beginning or a later section of the rally.

Rallymaster. The person or persons who lay out the rally. They set the perfect time, the mileage and all the course instructions.

Road rally. An automotive sport that is based on three basic principles of times, speed and distance.

Route instructions. The instructions given in the course map. Each section includes different types of route instructions such as tulip maps, string maps or calculations. A route instruction can also be a puzzle.

SCCA. Sports Car Club of America. This national group has created the Solo II rules that most event sponsoring clubs obey or adapt.

String map. Also known as a skeleton map or straight line map. The route instructions for string maps are slightly different: instead of being instructed to take a given road, you would be told to leave the opposing road behind.

TSD. Time, speed and distance, the basis of all rallies.

Tulip diagram. A type of route instruction that is entered at a "dot" and exited by an "arrow," unless otherwise stated in the general instructions.

WWV. A short wave radio signal that gives the exact time.

CHAPTER 3

Autocross
The Art of Solo II

*A*utocross offers all the thrills and fun of road racing at a fraction of the cost, with little risk. Autocross involves many of the same skills and techniques of road racing, on a smaller scale and at lower speeds. The pace is quick and maneuvers occur in rapid succession. A successful autocrosser has fast reflexes and good rhythm.

Autocross is an amateur sport on a national level. Competition is divided into classes, determined by the capability and preparation of your car. The classes are defined by the SCCA *Solo II* rule book. Other clubs also run autocrosses, and they usually follow SCCA Solo II rules as well.

Both slow and fast cars can be successful at autocross. Modern cars are small, light, and nimble. Today's manufacturers offer cars with responsive handling in addition to brute force. But older musclecars can be just as competitive and successful.

Autocross maneuvers will not harm a well-maintained car. Serious failures are rare, even in highly-modified high performance cars. The fastest drivers practice extremely smooth driving techniques. Abusing a car in an autocross run is inherently harmful to both the car and to your timed performance.

AUTOCROSS

Autocross is a family sport. Don't hesitate to bring your spouse or significant other. Even your children may participate if they are at least 16 years old, possess a valid drivers license, and sign a waiver.

If you are single, this is a great way to meet someone without social pressures. For starters, you'll both have cars and high speed events in common. If you are a car fanatic, this is another reason to try Solo II.

Female autocrossers can be just as competitive as their male rivals; they will equally enjoy learning and succeeding at something new.

Daily-driver car owners also aspire to test the limits of their cars.

The competition and fun of autocross is enhanced by more serious benefits. One such benefit is a knowledge of your car's characteristics and capabilities under stressful conditions. This can help any driver to avoid and recover from road hazards, having a practiced response for many different situations.

Autocross can make you a safer driver.

Solo Basics

Autocross, Solo II, *gymkhana*, and *slalom* racing are similar forms of amateur automobile racing. All are driven to compete for the lowest times around a defined obstacle course, one car at a time. Some include games and backing up.

Solo II is the most popular version. Solo II tests the driver's ability and the car's handling and agility on a short, structured course. Autocrosses

AUTOCROSS

are driven forward, at slow to medium speeds, through a course defined by rubber traffic *pylons*. Times are measured in hundredths of a second.

Where course conditions allow, more than one car can compete, if separated by adequate time and distance. Drivers may attain speeds of up to 70 mph. It is possible that speeds may not exceed 50 mph, depending on course layout.

Class winners are determined by the fastest time, minus penalties, comparing all cars in a given class with similar performance features.

A valid driver's license and a mechanically sound car (able to pass the safety inspection) are the only requirements for the Solo beginner. You must wear a helmet and a seatbelt at all times.

Competition licenses are not required for Solo II, and hazards do not exceed those encountered in normal daily driving.

Note from the outset that if an accident occurs, you will not be covered under your insurance policy. No passengers are allowed in the car, unless you are attending a driving school and a teacher is riding with you.

You may wish to attend an autocross event first, just to watch and ask questions. There is usually no charge to watch, and it's the best way to view this chapter in action.

There are other ways to sample autocross, or to brush up on your skills: some local SCCA regions offer driving schools once a year; other regions have $1 "fun runs" after an event, time permitting.

Before The Race

Registration

Most events start between 9:00 a.m. and 10:00 a.m. An early arrival will allow you proper time to prepare and walk the course.

AUTOCROSS

Park your car in an area designated for entrants, and unload your car to mark your spot. Then find the registration area and begin the entry procedures.

At registration, you will be asked to show your driver's license and SCCA membership card, if you have one. You will have to sign a waiver to clear the track and the host or sponsoring club of any liability. This is true at all sports events, due to the legal implications.

The registrar will hand you a form for tech inspection and registration, and will tell you where to park your car for the inspection.

Tech Inspection

Once you are in line at technical inspection, place your tech card on the dash or under the wipers so that it doesn't get lost, and open your hood. It is wise to stay with your car in line so the inspector can get started as soon as he or she comes to your car.

The inspector will check for basic safety (see tech inspection list).

Clean out all the extras--yes, even the tissue box. You never know when the "Attack of the Killer Kleenex" will unfold during an event. Anything moving around is a distraction and potentially dangerous.

You may leave your spare tire in the car. Some cars, like those with front engine, rear-wheel drives, need the extra weight in the rear. While some competitors may advise you to remove that spare, this may be a time when someone else's ideas do not work to your advantage.

The technical committee is empowered to declare ineligible for competition any vehicle which, in their opinion, would prove dangerous to the driver, other drivers, course workers or spectators.

AUTOCROSS

Tech Inspection List

Tips for a hassle-free inspection:

1. **Tires** should have approximately 25 percent of their tread. Cracks, tears, or retreads are not allowed; neither are nails or cuts in the tread. Repaired tires are not recommended.
2. **Wheels** should be free of cracks or damage.
3. The **steering and front end** should not have excessive play and should be in good working order. There should be no binding or looseness in the front end, including the wheel bearings, king pins, ball joints, or A-arms.
4. Factory **seat belts** must be securely mounted to the frame or floors, with no tears or damage. A five-point harness is optional. Shoulder harnesses are recommended.
5. **Fluid Leaks** of any kind are not allowed. A coolant catch can should be used on all cars.
6. **Brakes** should be in proper working order, with at least 50 percent of each brake pad remaining. Check for fluid leaks or cracks in the hoses, calipers, and rigid lines. Rotors should be within specifications, without cracks or damage.
7. Both interior and exterior of the vehicle should be free of **loose objects** that might dislodge and cause the driver to lose control of the vehicle. This includes the trunk and glove box. Wheel covers and hub caps must also be removed.
8. **Helmets** should be free of cracks or damage. Every competitor must have a helmet safety rated "Snell 85" or better.
9. Drivers of open cars must have **eye protection**: a face shield, goggles or similar face protection.
10. The **exhaust** should be intact and not hanging. Many locations have maximum decibel limits, so open exhausts aren't usually allowed.
11. The **battery** should be securely mounted with a proper hold-down device.

AUTOCROSS

Classification

Once your car passes technical inspection, which may include more details than listed above, the tech inspector will sign your card and place your car in a class based on its type and number of modifications. It is the driver's responsibility for car classification. Incorrect classification can be the cause of protest and possible disqualification.

Each car is classified with similar cars based on size and engine displacement.

Park your car and return to registration. The registrar will give you a choice of car numbers. It is wise to choose a later number to see how other drivers handle the course. Cars will run in numerical order, and this can be to your advantage. Try to select a number between 30 and 50.

After paying the entry fee, you will receive a packet with a map of the course, car numbers (sometimes numbers are written in white shoe polish), general rules, and any supplemental rules and regulations. Make sure you understand all the rules and regulations. Then be sure to walk the course.

Walking The Course

The most common mistake of a newcomer is getting lost on the course the first time out.

Make an effort to study the course map. The course will always begin with a set of timing lights. The start should be marked on your map.

While walking the course, be sure to note which pylons might not be visible when driving, because of their alignment. Walk with a more

AUTOCROSS

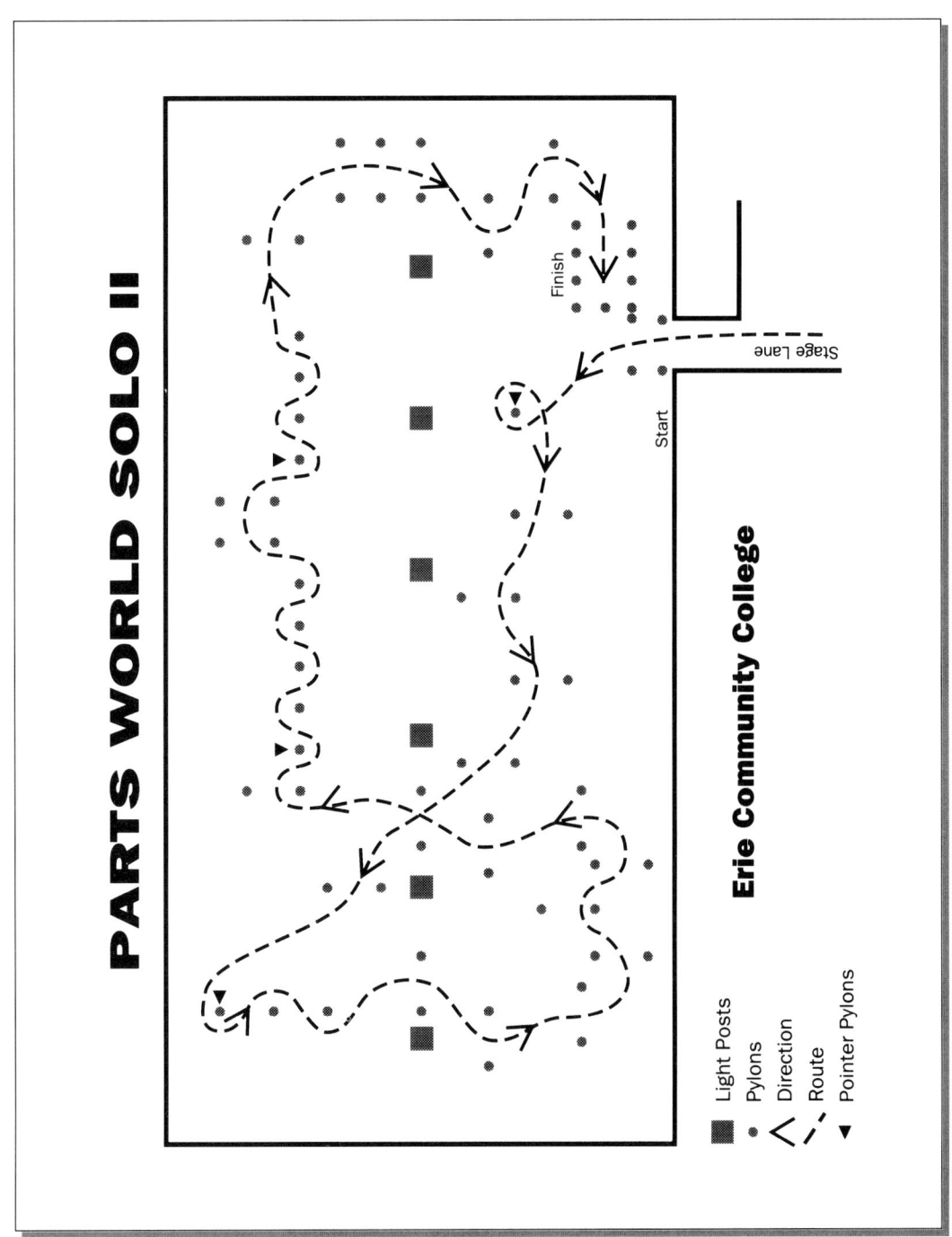

Sample course

AUTOCROSS

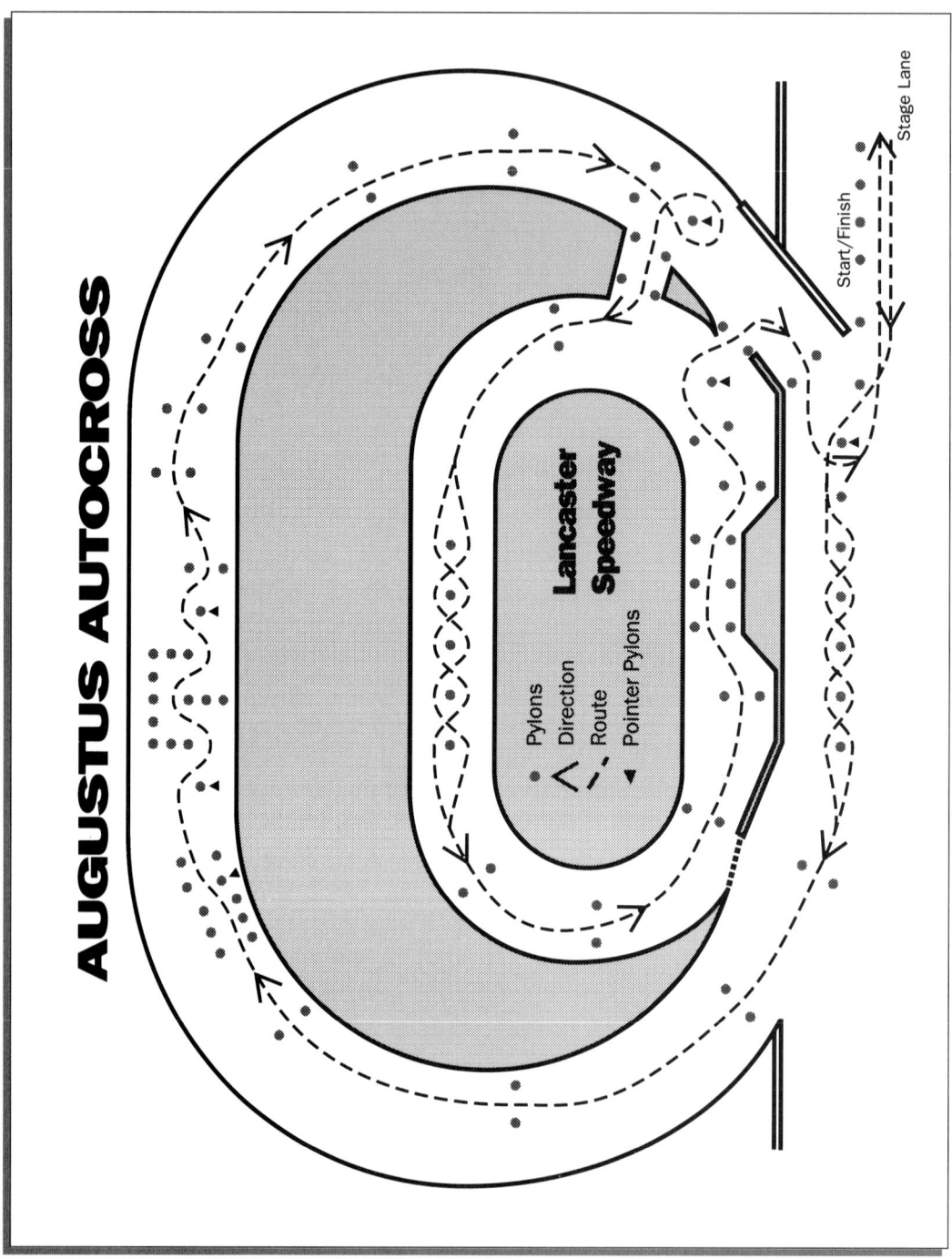

Sample course map

AUTOCROSS

experienced driver to pick up some clues. At weekend events, I've spent hours walking the same course so that I can be as competitive as possible.

Walk the course at least three times. The first time, memorize the layout of the course. The second, decide how to handle optional turns and how to take certain trouble areas like pin turns or blind corners. Finally, put it all together and think about the course to learn every little aspect. Memorize every turn and pylon. The course looks different when you're driving through it quickly, and the perspective changes.

Attend the drivers' meeting on time, and listen carefully. The event coordinators will introduce the *safety steward(s)* governing the event. This is the only real time to sort out any discrepancies or problems with the course. Voice any questions you might have about the event. If you have any confusion, don't hesitate to ask, especially where safety is involved.

Preparing For The Run

The event usually begins right after the drivers' meeting. They will usually call the first ten cars to the starting line. It is your responsibility to be in the proper numerical order at the start line when your car number is due.

There are usually five to ten cars waiting in line to start at any one time. If you fail to run in proper order, you could lose that run. After all the cars at the event have made their first run, the numerical sequence will begin again.

The only exception to the starting order would be a rerun, which is granted if there is a timing failure, if the course is obstructed and you are stopped by an official, or if a pylon is down by someone else's error. A rerun is not granted for

AUTOCROSS

OC (off course) runs, or if you knock down a pylon or stop for no reason.

Most events will allow you a minimum of three runs of the course. Some may have as many as five runs--based on the time allotted.

In The Driver's Seat

Seating position is important. The mind and the body work together, so comfort is necessary. You should feel comfortable, but not too relaxed.

The best way to see if you're positioned correctly is to cross your arms and place them on the steering wheel at the three and nine o'clock positions. Your arms should be straight or slightly bent. If they aren't, adjust your seat. Then place your hands normally on the wheel at three and nine. Your arms should be slightly bent and in a relaxed but aggressive position. Never let your elbow hang out the window.

Some competitors like to place their hands at ten and two. This is your choice, but I have found that three and nine are most effective.

Now check to see if your feet can fully engage all the pedals firmly. If not, you may have to make some adjustments for your seat. Try not to get too close or too far from the steering wheel.

Your hands should always be on the wheel. Never let your arm hang out the window. The only time your hands should leave the wheel, while on course, is to shift (and only for the time needed to shift). Riding the shift knob is not good for the transmission and you may lose control of the car.

The Starting Line

At the starting line, get prepared:
- *Tighten your seatbelt* to minimize driver movement. The lapbelt should be as tight as possible.

AUTOCROSS

- *Lock your doors* for a little extra rigidity.
- *Put on your helmet* and optional gloves.
- *Make sure your windows are down.*

The starter may check your vehicle again for basic safety items.

Remember how you plan to attack the course. When the starter tells you to go, take off, but don't leave rubber. Making all kinds of noise is a waste of time. Squeeze the pedal on and follow the correct path through the course.

A Quick Lesson In Handling

Handling can best be described as control. The more control, the better the handling. Speed is a basic function of handling: the better the handling, the safer the car at any speed. Obviously, any knowledge of handling will help you be more competitive.

All aspects of handling are based on the design of your car and are typically influenced by the original intended use of the car and its cost.

The first handling terms you need to know are *understeer* and *oversteer*. In simple terms, the words relate to which end of the car slips or loses traction faster in a turn. Understanding the difference is essential.

Understeer occurs when the front tires lose traction before the rear, causing a plowing or pushing effect. Such loss of traction can propel a car off the outside of a turn, giving the driver a frustrating loss of control.

Oversteer occurs when the rear tires lose traction first. The rear end tends to slide toward the outside of a turn. This can cause you to run off the inside of the curve, also known as spinning out. You will hear this expression quite often in the discussion of handling and speed.

Oversteer and understeer may both be corrected by *neutral steer*. This is when front and rear traction are matched. It can occur only at a certain speed on a given corner, with just the right combination of steering angle and throttle. While that may sound like a lot of variables, a practiced driver can make a car handle properly, if the chassis is set up properly. Neutral steer is a theory for baseline evaluation used for comparison. It cannot be consistently obtained.

Three other characteristics with which you should be familiar are squat, dive, and body roll.

Squat is the rearward weight transfer under acceleration that produces steering lightness. Dive is forward weight transfer under heavy braking, which may result in locking the rear brakes. Body roll basically describes itself. It can be felt during rapidly succeeding turns, as in a slalom, and is caused by centrifugal force.

These forces are usually experienced when a car is driven near its limit. Body roll tends to accentuate both understeer and oversteer.

For more information on the complex engineering science of handling, seek out a good handling book, the publications of suspension manufacturers, or an automotive trade magazine.

Three Basic Moves

Braking, turning, and accelerating are the only maneuvers you should think about on the course. This means that you will never coast between turns or in turns. It's either brake or gas--there is no in-between. You will stay on the gas until the last possible moment.

Smoothness counts. When you step on the gas or the brakes, pretend there is an egg under the pedal. If you push down too hard, too fast, you

AUTOCROSS

will have egg all over your shoes. Then ease the brakes off slowly as you get into the turn.

Drive through the corner, close to or at the limit of adhesion. Always take the path that is straightest through the corner. This will give you the least resistance. If you overdrive the course, or go beyond the limit of adhesion, you will lose speed and control.

An expression used in road racing fits the cornering situation perfectly: "Enter a corner slower and you will be able to exit the corner quicker."

Try to keep the car balanced between the front and rear as much as possible. Don't overdrive the car at any time. If your front tires slide and you overcorrect or oversteer farther than necessary, you will definitely slow down. It won't do much for your tires either.

Front wheel drive cars are quite competitive.

Speed on course will be added naturally as you become a better autocrosser. If you add speed too quickly and in the wrong areas, the runs that seem faster to you will actually be slower. Watch your competitors and see if you can tell when they are pushing too hard.

Show-offs only scrub off speed and transmit to the pavement half the power the car is capable of delivering. Again, smoothness and speed are the secrets to winning your class.

AUTOCROSS

Penalties

Penalties are based on the displacement of pylons. Two seconds are added to your total course time for each pylon that is displaced. This penalty may vary in some local regions.

Pylons are marked with two lines, one at the base, and one two inches away from the base. The outer edge of the line is the penalty limit. If the pylon is totally displaced or knocked over, the penalty is assessed.

Failure to follow the prescribed course will earn you an OC, and no time for your run will be listed on the scoreboard. If your run is off course or you are unable to continue, your score will read as DNF (did not finish). A course deviation will not be charged as an OC if the car hits a marker defining course limits.

DNS (did not start) means that you missed your turn to run.

Each driver gets three timed runs, with the best of the three counting for class position.

At the conclusion of your run, you will have either a stop box or a running finish. A running finish will allow you to accelerate through the stop line to break the timing light beam, then stop as quickly and safely as possible. If the course concludes with a stop box, you must stop the car within the stop box without knocking over any of the pylons defining that box.

Pylons at the stop box usually carry twice the penalty of a pylon on course. If you come flying into the stop box and knock over the last center pylon, you will definitely be penalized. But if the pylon is leaning on your car, it is smart to back up a little in order to stand up the pylon and avoid the penalty.

AUTOCROSS

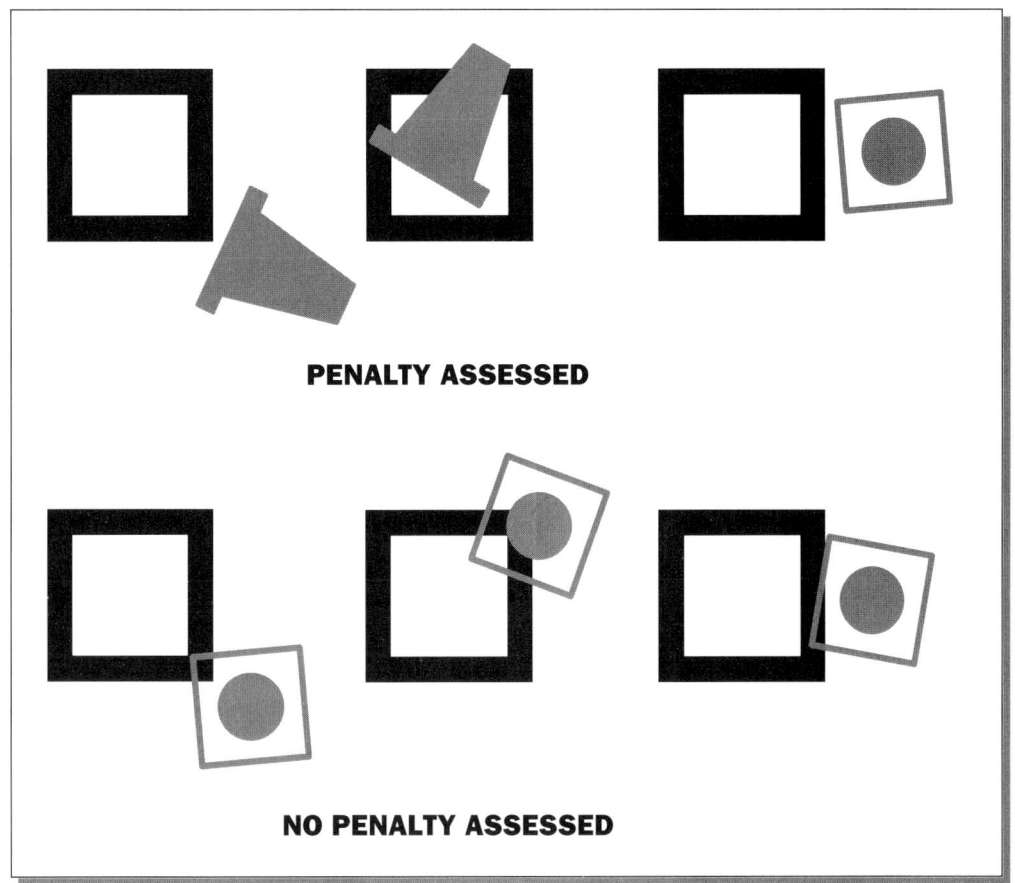

PENALTY ASSESSED

NO PENALTY ASSESSED

Penalties are posted with official times. An "X" or "|" will indicate a pylon displaced on a particular run. There will be one mark for each pylon. The times posted are not considered official until verified by the chief scorer.

Course Marshals

While you are on course, you will be observed by course marshals and course workers. The marshals are the final authority if there are any questions about penalties, and their decisions cannot be overturned. They will record any

AUTOCROSS

knocked-down pylons or instances of not following the course layout.

Each course marshal's station will have a fire extinguisher and a red flag to serve as a warning device should some danger exist to you while on course. If you should ever have the red flag waved at you, stop your car immediately and wait for further instructions from the course marshal. You will then be entitled to a rerun.

The Finish

Once you are across the finish line, your run is over. You should slow down as quickly as possible and return to your pit or parking area.

There are usually participants and spectators in the pits, including children, so use common sense and drive slowly. It is also very important to remember not to run over the timing equipment located at the finish line. Failure to slow to a safe speed can result in an immediate disqualification and a lecture from the solo safety steward.

Once you have completed your run, an unofficial time should be posted on the scoreboard. It usually takes a little time to be posted.

Do not attempt to get your time directly from the timing team. This causes confusion for the timers (who are instructed not to give out times anyway), and can cause a safety hazard. Be patient. Your results will be posted in due time.

At the end of the event, trophies and scores will be handed out and announced by the *event chairman*. A copy of the scores are usually mailed to you or printed in that club's next newsletter.

If you drive off course or have a slow run, do not let it bother you. You will have two or three more runs to get it the way you want it. So never let a bad run get you down. Just try again.

AUTOCROSS

You should analyze your bad run, figure out where you went wrong, then correct it next time out. If you spun out, you have just learned the maximum adhesion or the limit of your car--a very good lesson.

You can never practice too much. The more you take part in Solo II, the better you will drive. Eventually, winning will be second nature.

Working The Course

If your region requires you to work the course in-between runs, you should contact the course marshal in charge of *course work* as soon as possible so you do not miss your next run.

"Working the course" means that you are temporarily appointed to be a course marshal, to work a segment of the course, and to write down any penalties that occur during the time you worked. You will be relieved from working in a short period of time, as long as everyone who finishes their run works the course immediately after finishing.

Advanced Lessons

The Human Factor

You may be saying, "Solo II sure sounds fun, and I'm sure it would make me a better driver. But I'll probably be last in my class and make a fool of myself."

Along with educating you on the basics, let's start you off on the right foot toward winning your class. Here are a few secrets to make you even more competitive, and a few tips for psyching out the competition.

Car and driver preparation are extremely important. Knowing your personal limitations and your car's mechanical limitations is the start of

AUTOCROSS

A sports car enthusiast tests his responses and the car's limits.

becoming a better and more competitive driver. As you increase your knowledge of driving, your concept car and driver will also improve. With increased experience you will be able to go faster. The mind and the body must work in harmony to have quick reflexes and responses.

Wear your most comfortable clothes--jeans and a T-shirt--because fashion is not important. Do not wear anything that is binding or restrictive to your movement, especially to the arms. Sneakers or a comfortable pair of shoes should be worn. Do not wear open-toed shoes or sandals. Driving gloves can be beneficial. You'll get a better grip on the steering wheel and the shift knob.

Try to learn from your competitors. Observe them on course, and note how they drive the course differently. You can pick up a few tips on driving a similar vehicle. Soon you too will be a trophy collector. Experience comes with regular autocross participation--the more the better.

Psychological Strategy

The psychological factor is also important, so mental preparation before an event can be helpful. Everyone has their own way of doing this. Some people need only the excitement of the event to get psyched up. Pretending to be Mario or A.J. enroute to the event is a poor idea. Don't develop a bad attitude by trying to impress yourself or other competitors with driving heroics before or after an event. The place to prove yourself is on the course.

AUTOCROSS

Your times will speak for themselves.

There are many psyche-out maneuvers that can be fun, but they should not be attempted until you have progressed in the sport. You must become a better driver to be any kind of threat to your competition.

Get a good start with no alcohol the night before, followed by a full night's sleep.

Walk the course three or four times to let others know that you are serious, and you plan to be as competitive as possible. They will definitely not think of you as a novice.

If your main competitor is psyching you out, try to do the same. Get a spiral note pad and pen and, as the competitor gets his or her car teched, take notes, even if it's just doodles. Make the other driver think you are taking notes on items that are not allowed and considered cheating. If he or she *is* cheating, they will suspect you might file a protest and turn them in. This can be distracting, and you have turned the tables.

I have also written strange numbers on my tires to make others believe they are my tire pressures. If they ask, we tell them the numbers have no meaning. I definitely do not want to hurt anybody, or cause a blowout. Use your head and you will see all kinds of tricks used by other participants.

I don't condone cheating or false protests. Only jerks protest people for poorly-based reasons. It won't help you, and it will ruin the spirit of the event and your reputation. Psyching out is a talent and a fun source of mischief; it is not meant to be devious, unsafe, or malicious.

Adjust Your Start

Beginning at the starting line, it is not necessary to line up straight on to the starting pylons. You can adjust the car to the right or the

AUTOCROSS

left of the start line area. Watch other competitors line up to get the best angle on the first set of pylons. When leaving the start line, accelerate quickly, but just short of spinning your tires.

Time Your Shifting

Shifting with an automatic is not always necessary, unless you are in a tight corner. Never use the transmission to keep the engine near its torque peak or red line. Some engines produce their best torque at lower rpms.

In Solo II, torque is more important than horsepower. Torque gives you acceleration without reaching your top speed.

It is most important to shift at the right time, as smoothly and quickly as possible. Your hands should never leave the wheel except during shifting, and only for the brief amount of time needed to shift. Do not grind a pound of gear --they don't make rubber gears yet! When entering a corner you want to be in the right gear before you start to brake.

You can use any of these techniques in everyday driving on city streets.

Always shift down or up while driving in a straight line, because shifting in a corner can cause a spin or loss of control. A sudden downshift can cause the rearend to break loose and unsettle the suspension.

You will sometimes have to decide whether to shift at the end of a straight or hold the engine at redline to save a second. Again, every time you shift you lose a second, but do not blow up your engine to save a second.

Brake Smoothly

Braking is used to slow the car, but spend as little time as possible braking. This does not mean to jab the brakes.

Threshold braking is the type of braking used

in Solo II and other types of racing. It can be described as the maximum deceleration obtained by braking as hard as possible, just prior to locking up the wheels. Brake rapidly, smoothly, and only while driving in a straight line.

Don't be afraid to brake hard, but never lock them up. Brake lockup will leave you with no steering, no handling, and no control. If you have anti-lock brakes (ABS), you will be unable to lock your brakes. That can be a great advantage.

Accelerate At The Apex

There are many differently-shaped corners on an autocross course: fast, slow, tight, open, decreasing or increasing radius, slalom and pin turns. Refer to chapter four for diagrams illustrating these corners.

Two important cornering terms are *apex* and *balancing point.* The apex is the point where the car is closest to the inside, or the peak, of the corner. The balancing point is the point of transition from deceleration to acceleration.

Always take the straightest path through a corner to make the corner as flat as possible. This will give you the least resistance. For example, enter an L-shaped turn a little slower so that you can start to accelerate at the apex of the corner. Smoothly apply the gas until you reach the exit.

When driving through a slalom, try to just miss the pylon. Keep the pylon as close as possible to the left door in left turns and the right door in right turns. Steer into turns and accel- erate between pylons.

Be sure to note distances by counting paces between each pylon in your initial walk through the course. This will help you figure the spacing of the pylons ahead of time.

Turn the steering wheel as little as possible. I like to turn the wheel 90 degrees between each turn unless the pylons get progressively closer or wider.

AUTOCROSS

Try to get a smooth rhythm between the turns and straighten out the corners as much as possible. Do not try to gain time in tight areas; time can be gained between maneuvers, or in wider corners.

Another type of corner you may encounter is a pin turn. These sharp turns can be tricky if not approached properly.

The best way to attack pin turns is to brake heavily before entering the pin turn, drive it around, then accelerate hard out of the turn. If you step on the gas too soon, or try to push the car around the pin too fast, you will just plow your car straight ahead and make a large loop that will actually slow you down. It is faster to stay closer to the pylon and drive slowly.

Tips For Better Vehicle Performance

Now that you are prepared, what about the car? It is wise to get a fresh tune-up. This can help your car respond as well as you do.

Go through the safety check list. Check for vacuum or fluid leaks. Tighten lug studs and nuts to shop manual specifications. If any are broken or missing, be sure to make repairs before the event. The organizers simply will not let you compete if your vehicle is unsafe.

Brakes are a safety item that many people pass up. If your brake calipers fail at speed, you will not soon forget it. Such failures always come as a surprise, and do not make your weekend more pleasant. Check your brake calipers, hose, pads, hard lines, master cylinder, and linings. Change your brake fluid before each event.

I like to say that not checking your brakes is like not folding your parachute properly: You take your chances.

AUTOCROSS

Customize Your Handling

Adjustment	To Increase: Understeer	Oversteer
Front tire pressure	lower	higher
Rear tire pressure	higher	lower
Front tire section	smaller	larger
Rear tire section	larger	smaller
Front wheel camber	more positive	more negative
Rear wheel camber	more negative	more positive
Front springs	stiffer	softer
Rear springs	softer	stiffer
Front anti-sway bar	thicker/stiffer	thinner/softer
Rear anti-sway bar	thinner/softer	thicker/stiffer
Weight distribution	more forward	more rearward

Handling

You can always make a car handle to your taste. The simplest and cheapest method is the addition of air pressure to your tires. Everyone does it--you'll notice your competition constantly increasing, decreasing, checking, and testing tire pressures.

Increasing tire pressures keeps your tires from deforming or rolling under during hard cornering, and can be effective in reducing understeer and oversteer. The general rule is to put the air where the action is: in front to reduce understeer, and in the rear to reduce oversteer.

Air is nearly free, but there are slightly more expensive ways to improve your car's handling characteristics. Aftermarket springs, sway bars, shocks, high performance tires, and polyurethane bushings are the best components to start with,

AUTOCROSS

especially if you find yourself approaching autocross as a full-time hobby.

There is no way to get the exact feel of the autocross course without attempting it yourself. But we will attempt to get you and your car ready so you can derive the most enjoyment out of autocross. With all the information we have already discussed in mind, we now can apply it to the course.

Experience, The Final Factor

Armed with this chapter's information, you can drive any course and think about how to improve your time, every time. Keep in mind where you will shift and brake, and where you made mistakes in previous runs. You may find the difference between your time and competitors' times to be as little as one-hundredth of a second, and seldom more than a couple of seconds. Obviously, this means you must make fewer mistakes to win your class.

Now you are no longer a rookie. You are ready to go out and drive the course with a little edge on the competition. You now know secrets that many autocrossers won't figure out for years. Still, I must warn you. Solo II events can become an addiction. It's a fun one, though, and it only gets better from here.

AUTOCROSS GLOSSARY

Italicized words found in this chapter:

Apex. A point along a curve or corner where the largest possible radius touches the inside edge of the turn.

Autocross. An amateur automobile sport, in which competitors drive a prescribed closed course, where the fastest time in a particular class of cars wins.

Balancing point. The point of transition from deceleration to acceleration.

Competitor. A qualified driver who has started at least one run at an event, with a safety-teched car.

Course work. Some regions require competitors to work the course when not actually competing. This includes picking up pylons, noting penalties on the course, and assisting in any way.

DNS. Did not start. If a competitor is unable to run a round, for any reason, DNS notes that run's score (equal to zero).

Event chairman. The person in charge of the event, responsible for designing, laying out, and pre-running the course; enforces compliance with Solo II rules and regulations.

Gymkhana. Similar to Solo II, but generally a level-ground contest that involves obstacles, forward and reverse maneuvers, cloverleaf turns, parking, and garaging exercises, with a time and penalty scoring system.

Neutral Steer. When a car does not oversteer or understeer and all four wheels have similar sliding characteristics.

OC. Off course. When a car has left the prescribed course at some time during a run, or all four wheels are off the track surface.

Oversteer. When rear tires lose traction before the front tires. The rear end will tend to slide toward the outside of a turn.
Penalties. Assessed when a pylon is moved out of its marked box, or is knocked over. Each pylon is equivalent to two seconds added to a score.
Pylons. Rubber cone markers used to delineate a course.
Safety steward. The individual with primary responsibility for event safety. This includes course security, driver and worker safety, and spectator safety.
Slalom. An event similar to an autocross, though its course may be one serpentine portion of a gymkhana or autocross layout.
Solo II. An event generally held on a paved, flat surface. The course generally consists of straight sections and connecting turns and corners, resembling a miniaturized road course. The course layout should emphasize car handling skill and maneuverability rather than performance.
Threshold braking. A method of braking quickly without locking. Force is applied firmly, to a position just prior to lockup.
Understeer. When front tires lose traction before the rear tires, causing a plowing or pushing effect.

CHAPTER 4

Driving Schools
"So You Want To Drive In The Fast Lane?"

Now that you own a performance car, you probably think you know how to drive it. You've been inspired by that feeling of hitting a corner at a certain angle, or carrying a few more miles per hour through a highway bend. But the truth is that most drivers do not have solid knowledge of the capabilities and limitations of either themselves or their cars. They've found a few more thrills than before, and surprise themselves with the occasional handling trick. But they aren't really sure why it worked.

Before you decide to modify your car, or push it to the outer limits on some remote stretch of curving road, you should learn how to drive it more effectively. I'm not talking about high school driver's education, when the teacher screamed at you to turn left, stop there, and "DON'T DO THAT!" I'm talking about driving more effectively at high speeds without bringing harm to yourself or your investment. This is driving instruction the driver's ed. student never dreamed about.

Beyond the valuable instruction they provide, *driving schools* are a great, low-cost route to big league race tracks. Imagine being able to pull on a safety-rated helmet, get into your performance car, and drive onto such fabled tracks as Lime

DRIVING SCHOOLS

Rock Park in Connecticut, Charlotte Motor Speedway in North Carolina, Sebring in Central Florida, Laguna Seca and Sears Point in Northern California, Nelson Ledges in Ohio, or Watkins Glen International in Central New York. You can experience that hallowed pavement without suffering the expenses and perils of all-out racing.

This Is Not A Race

Driving schools are high-speed events, but no competition is involved. The intention is to teach you to drive your car safely at high speeds. This is the best place to discover whether racing cars as an amateur or professional is right for you.

You will be separated into class groups based on previous experience--everyone has to be a novice at least once. But there are never trophies awarded nor times posted. Learning to drive fast and safely are the key objectives.

The thrill of driving a bonafide racing circuit is a great feeling everyone should experience at least once. It sharpens your awareness of the car and makes you a safer street driver.

Simply put, high-speed events are an opportunity for you to drive your car at the speeds it was made for, under the safest conditions possible. The idea is to have fun while learning your car's abilities and expanding your own skills.

Qualified and experienced instructors are supplied to accompany you in the car at-speed, and to instruct you in the ways of driving quickly without screwing up. They start you slowly and allow you to progress at a safe, comfortable rate, with encouragement to improve your technique and confidence.

Instructors want to make sure you get your money's worth--they also want you back, so they want you to have fun. It is not unusual for students to attend several different schools a year,

DRIVING SCHOOLS

especially if they are held at different venues. Improvement is always possible.

There are many professional and amateur driving schools available, as well as club-sponsored instructional events at major tracks in the United States and Canada. The schools will give you an enormous increase in performance knowledge. Their driving and handling tips will transform your car into a performer, with increased longevity.

All of the principles of Solo II come together as a good base for driving schools. Solo II is a similar idea at much slower speeds. Do not let this talk of increased speed and danger scare you. Most people are a little nervous at the outset of a new challenge. As your knowledge increases, however, the nervousness will be replaced by a professional mindset concerned with safety and technique.

School Choice

With so many schools available in all areas of the country and the world, your selection should be an adventure in itself. Costs vary widely from school to school, as do the courses of instruction. Obviously, the more professional the approach, the more expensive the course.

Clubs sponsor events that are both affordable and instructive.

One of the very best schools for the money is TrackTime Performance Driving Schools, Inc., based out of Youngstown, Ohio. Their sessions are

This is a driving school at Mid-Ohio Road Course. Many different types of cars can be seen at these events.

DRIVING SCHOOLS

usually held over weekends, and their annual schedule takes them to numerous, well-established tracks in the northeast, midwest and south, plus occasional dates in Northern and Southern California. The instruction strikes a realistic balance between classroom and track time in the driver's seat.

If your long-term goal is to go racing, there are a number of specialized schools to suit your needs and your newly-attained levels of expertise. But TrackTime is a good place to start, to see if all-out racing is for you.

Refer to chapter seven for a directory of driving schools located throughout the United States.

A Few Ground Rules

All drivers must be at least 18 years of age, and must have a valid drivers license. All drivers must sign appropriate insurance waivers.

Your car must be pre-teched before attending the school. It will be briefly re-teched at the event.

As an entrant, you assume all risks of damage to persons and property during the event, when driving your car.

Long sleeves and long pants are required, and a driver's suit is optional. Driving gloves may help you get a better grip on the wheel.

Helmets must be rated "Snell 85" or better. Helmets will be teched with your car, and a tech sticker may be put on it.

Most events will be run rain or shine, though fog may cause a delay.

A schedule will be handed to every student. Most are followed closely, so count on the stated times. The schedule will list your group, classroom, and where to go. Keep the schedule with you at all times.

DRIVING SCHOOLS

Students may not take passengers on the track, except instructors. This is a strict insurance regulation.

Anyone repeatedly driving in a unsafe manner or ignoring the track rules will be ejected from the event without refund.

School Prep

You will generally receive a confirmation letter or packet about one month prior to your event date. Depending on the school, the packet may include instructions about who to contact when you arrive, general information on area hotels, directions to the track, driving rules and flag usage, a tech form and information sheet, a medical information form, and a track map.

After paying the entry fee, a few basics are required of prospective students. You will need a helmet rated Snell 85 or better, natural fiber long pants, and long-sleeved shirt. Nomex racing suits are not required, nor are roll cages, fuel cells, or other race equipment. As long as your car is equipped with the proper safety equipment, it is legal for driving schools or high-speed events.

Tech Inspection

Once you arrive at a school, the safety or tech inspection should be a simple formality because you or your mechanic will have thoroughly inspected your car before leaving home. A tech list is usually provided in the confirmation package sent by the event organizers.

Tech inspectors are not able to spend the time on your car that you might. It is your responsibility to put a safe car on the track.

If no such list is made available, you can refer to the list on the following page.

A special sticker is usually placed on a car after inspection, to assure that the car has passed

DRIVING SCHOOLS

Drivers School Tech Inspection List

1. **Tires** should have at least half of the original tread and no less than 3/32-inch of tread, must clear the suspension and fender edges, and be "S" rated (112 MPH) or better. Sidewalls must be in good condition, with no foreign objects lodged in the tread. Plugged or patched tires are not recommended. No bias-ply tires are allowed.
2. **Brakes** must have at least 50 percent of original material. Semi-metallic pads are recommended. Brake calipers, hoses and lines must be undamaged. Rotors should be within specifications. Flush lines with fresh brake fluid before each event.
3. **Steering** should not have excessive play. Power steering should be free of leaks. Front-wheel drive cars should check CV joints for leaks, and CV joint boot damage.
4. **Wheels** must be free of cracks or damage. Torque wheel lugs to proper specifications. No hub caps or trim rings allowed.
5. Original **seatbelts or race harnesses** are required, in good condition, with no cuts or frays, and mounted securely. Your passenger/instructor will also need belts. Shoulder harnesses are recommended.
6. **Battery** terminals must be tight, in good condition, and taped. The battery must be securely mounted and have no leaks.
7. Have at least one rearview **mirror**; two are recommended.
8. **The engine compartment** must be free of leaks, including anti-freeze, fuel, and oil. A radiator catch can is required.
9. **Trunk:** Spare tires and jacks may be removed or securely tightened down. Some schools require removal, others make it your choice.
10. No loose objects are allowed in the **interior.** Remove anything that could shift if your car is upside down. A fire extinguisher, preferably Halon, must be securely bracket-mounted.
11. Window **glass** should not be cracked or broken.
12. The entire **exhaust system** must be in good condition and securely mounted. Most events do not allow open exhausts. Tuneable mufflers are normally allowed.
13. **Open cars:** Some clubs require roll bars while others want the top up or down. Check with the chief tech inspector.

DRIVING SCHOOLS

Drivers School

TECHNICAL INSPECTION FORM

Name _____

Make of Car _____

Year _____ Model _____ Displ _____

License Plate No. _____ State _____

(*Initial Each*)

_____	TIRES - minimum tread 3/32" Sidewall condition, etc. Minimum pressure of 32 lbs.	_____	Brake lights & turn signals
		_____	Seat Belts (Driver & Passenger)
_____	BRAKES - pedal rims, check pad thickness if possible	_____	Exhaust system
_____	BRAKE FLUID - topped up & clear. changed in last 6 months	_____	Windshield (no major cracks)
		_____	Battery secure
_____	SHOCKS in good condition	_____	No fluid leaks (gas, oil, brake fluid)
_____	Steering linkage adjustment	_____	Throttle returns freely
_____	Wheel bearings properly adjusted	_____	Front Suspension top mounts condition
_____	Brake Dust Shields (MUST BE REMOVED)	_____	Motor mounts

The above car was inspected and found to be in compliance with the requirements set forth above.

Date _____

Signature of Inspector _____

Location _____

I acknowledge that the technical inspection performed upon my automobile is solely for the purpose of meeting minimum standards for car preparation for the Drivers School and no representation is made by the inspectors, or any other inspector selected by me, of road worthiness or fitness for general street driving or driving on Watkins Glen Road Course. No warranties are implied or expressed in passing or failing the inspection performed. I release the inspectors from any and all liability arising from their inspection whether or not due to their negligence. I acknowledge that all times I remain solely responsible for the safety and roadworthiness of my automobile and am not relying upon the inspection made in deciding whether or not to drive my automobile.

Signed _____

Date _____

DRIVING SCHOOLS

tech. Schools usually place a non-removable sticker on your windshield, that can be scraped off after the event. A smaller sticker is also placed on your helmet, to show it has cleared tech.

Insurance waivers must be signed at the entrance to the track and at the registration area. School officials will check again at the drivers meeting to ensure everyone has signed waivers. You must cooperate, as this is required by the insurance carrier backing the event.

The Drivers Meeting

Once your car is considered trackworthy, you are ready to attend your first driving school. Many people just walk in with no real idea what to expect. The brochures and fliers only give the "big picture." Let's preview what you can expect to see and learn.

Always attend the preliminary drivers meeting, no matter what you are doing. This meeting is required attendance at all driving schools. Some schools will not allow you on the track unless you have attended their safety and drivers meetings, and the ongoing classroom sessions.

Believe it or not, it is easy to miss a meeting if you are working on a car with a problem. Make sure that you keep the day's schedule with you at all times. Most schools run on time and, if you're not where you are supposed to be, you'll only short-change yourself by missing class or track time you've already paid for.

The typical drivers meeting stresses both your safety and your fun. The information includes the makeup of the run groups, an introduction of the instructors, a rundown on current track conditions, track characteristics known to experienced drivers, and any schedule changes.

The drivers meeting will talk about pre-grid

DRIVING SCHOOLS

(where to position your car in preparation for going on the track) and where to pick up and drop off your assigned instructor. Still, there is more you will need to know before getting on the track.

Classroom Instruction

Some schools offer a track familiarization ride with your instructor after the drivers meeting. Most schools send the beginners to a classroom session to better prepare them for this new experience. School officials understand that this is an exciting event. Their goals are to inform you of the basics and calm you down so that you can think about the information given in the classroom session.

Drivers with previous performance experience will probably be placed in the first grouping of cars headed for the track. They'll be making all the noise while you sit in a classroom, but you'll get your turn.

Instructors ride side-saddle to assist you around the course.

The classroom session will teach beginners the theory and methods of proper and safe driving. They will also teach you to drive safely in a controlled environment where you can concentrate on sharpening your driving skills. The schools strive to provide both an excellent learning experience and an enjoyable one. You will never be pushed to do anything you feel uncomfortable with or do not understand.

You will be grouped with people of similar experience for the classroom and track sessions. Groups can be sectioned into three or four levels of expertise, depending on the track organizers

DRIVING SCHOOLS

Stay in your assigned class for the whole event. Even if you understand the basics, you might miss details taught to that first group that you will need to know in an advanced class.

and the club or business. Basically, participants are divided into beginner, intermediate, and experienced drivers. You will remain in your assigned group unless an organizer or instructor feels it wise to move you.

Flagging procedures

Flags are used on the track to inform drivers of any information that could affect their car or their course at or before the next corner. Each corner has a safety location run by a person called a *corner worker*. Corner workers will be the only people with flags except at the start/finish line.

Flags may be displayed either stationary or waving. If a flag is waving, the condition is immediately ahead. Remember, this is the only communication the track officials and corner workers have with drivers. These standard flags and flagging procedures are used at each event unless stated otherwise at the drivers meeting:

Green. The course is clear and the event is underway.

Yellow. Take care, no passing, or a hazardous condition is ahead. Reduce speed. If the flag is waving, a hazard may exist before the next corner station.

Yellow with vertical red stripes. Take care, a slippery condition is ahead--possibly oil or coolant on the track. Slow down; if the flag is waving, be prepared to stop. No passing is allowed.

Red. Stop as soon as possible and wait for instructions.

Black. If the flag is pointed directly at your car, come in on the next lap and report to the track official.

Black with a red dot (meatball). A mechanical

DRIVING SCHOOLS

failure or problem has been noticed on your car by a corner worker or track official. Pull into the pits as soon as possible to meet with a track official and a tech inspector.

Blue with yellow diagonal stripe. If this flag is stationary, let the faster car pass. Follow the passing rules, and permit the pass at the next designated location. Some schools just use a solid blue flag. If the flag is waving, check your mirrors immediately, because someone is coming up fast.

Memorize this list. The same flags are used in amateur racing.

White/white with a red cross. An emergency vehicle is on the track. Slow down, don't pass, and be prepared to stop.

Checkered flag. Your session is complete. Slow down to cool the car, and pull into the pits at the first possible chance.

Track Rules

This list of rules is standard for most tracks. Each school or club event may vary in the details. Even after you have studied the list, be sure to read the general driving rules for every event.

Conduct. Students or guests consuming drugs or alcohol while the school is in session will be asked to leave the track.

Passing. Pass another car only when you receive an arm signal from that driver. Pass with the correct passing signal--the left hand outside the window of the car being overtaken. Check each event for passing on the right or left sides.

Do not try to pass at the end of the straights.

If the car being passed does not see you, it is acceptable to flash your lights. The instructor in the car being overtaken may be explaining something to the student, and you may have to wait for the next passing zone.

DRIVING SCHOOLS

Use your mirrors. If a car is overtaking you, or is faster in the corners, signal that car to pass. When you are being passed, ease off the gas. No side-by-side racing is allowed down the straights or through the corners.

Special situations will be covered at the drivers meeting.

Following. Do not bunch in groups. If you find yourself in a group, pull into the pits and ask to be restarted.

Do not tailgate other students. Back off and wait for a passing zone, then wait for the passing signal. Do not pass after the checkered flag has been given.

Flags. Note the corner worker stations for communication with the flags. Standard flags will be used and discussed in drivers' meetings.

At the conclusion of your session, a checkered flag will be displayed. Enter the pits at the first possible opportunity. Do not run an extra lap.

If you are given a black flag or a meatball flag, be sure to acknowledge the flag by waving your hand at the corner worker. Pull into the pits as soon as possible. Someone will be waiting for you.

If a red flag is displayed at any station, stop as quickly and as safely as you can. Keep in mind that other cars are behind you. Pull off to the edge of the track until further instructions are given.

Tracktime

In The Driver's Seat

Seating position is extremely important. Improper seating can inhibit your driving ability and your view of happenings around you. Feedback

You will learn techniques of both solo and group driving.

DRIVING SCHOOLS

from the car is felt through the steering wheel, brake pedal, driver's seat, and by sight and sounds. Be constantly aware of these signals--it's the way the car communicates with you.

Your seating position should not be too close to the wheel. While sitting close may seem to offer a better view, you will lose a certain amount of freedom of movement. If the seat is too relaxed--too far back--then you will lose vision and control.

Dig your body all the way back. Do not sit on the seat, sit *in* the seat. Become part of the seat. When everything is adjusted properly, your shoulders should not break contact with the seat and your arms and legs should be slightly bent.

Adjust the seat so that all pedals can be fully engaged. Then adjust the seat back so that, with your hands on the steering wheel at positions three and nine o'clock, your arms are slightly bent and do not touch the back of the seat.

An instructor shows safety features of race cars to a student.

It is essential that a driver remain firmly seated. Seatbelts should be tightened properly. If you are using factory belts, be sure to tighten the lap belt across your waist, not your stomach. Make the lap belt as tight as possible without cutting off circulation. It should not cause discomfort.

The shoulder belt should be as tight as possible. Always tighten shoulder harnesses last. If you are using a race harness, always tighten the lap belts first, then adjust the anti-submarine belts (if you are using them), but do not allow the lap belts to slip off your hips. Finally, tighten down the shoulder harnesses.

DRIVING SCHOOLS

Starting Off Slowly

When you finally get on the track, do not expect to drop your right foot immediately to the floor. The car may not be warmed up completely and, obviously, it is not smart to push a cold engine. Wait for the car to reach proper operating temperature before testing rev limits and acceleration rates.

You'll also need to warm up your tires. Soon after beginning to drive the track, test your brakes and steering, but watch for other cars.

Take time to familiarize yourself with the track, corner stations, corner names, and the cones or pylons placed on or adjacent to the track. Cones are usually set out to represent the *entry*, *apex*, and *exit* of each corner, so that the track is safer for you and other drivers.

Remember, speed comes naturally with experience. Always learn the line first, then gradually add the speed.

There are many aspects of high-speed driving, and this book can only give a taste of what to expect and what to do. A number of books have been written on handling and handling factors, including tire adhesion, slip angles, *neutral steer*, understeer, *oversteer*, four- wheel drift, balance, and weight transfer. All these topics are usually covered in detail in your classroom sessions.

Pedal Power

There may be as many as four pedals that you will need to deal with. The gas pedal is the easy one, and smoothness counts here as well. Push it

DRIVING SCHOOLS

downward as if there were an egg under the pedal that you do not want to crush on the carpet.

The most powerful part of the car is the brakes, not the engine, and brakes can be used to your advantage. Proper braking starts with threshold braking, slowing the car as quickly as possible with a firm pedal, without locking the wheels. If you have an anti-lock braking system you will not be able to lock your brakes anyway.

Never slam on your brakes. If your wheels are locked you will lose control, which can be scary and dangerous. Sudden, hard braking causes weight to transfer forward to the front wheels. That puts all the braking effort on the front brakes, and causes the car to be out of balance.

To brake properly, apply increasing pressure, squeezing down gently but firmly. Be tough on the brakes, but do not push them to the point of lock-up. Think of it as a hug.

Of course, your brake pedal should be firm and hard at all times. If that is not the case, there may be a malfunction.

The clutch pedal is to be used only when shifting. Do not ride the clutch or leave your foot on the pedal. This will only wear down the clutch prematurely. You should know exactly the point where your clutch grabs, and develop a touch for it. When shifting, move the lever as quickly as possible and get your hand back on the wheel.

The fourth pedal is also referred to as a "dead pedal" or brace pedal. It is positioned to the far left and gives a driver lateral support while cornering. If you do not presently have one, it is definitely worth your while to install one. Once you try it, you won't believe how much it helps keep you in your seat in corners.

DRIVING SCHOOLS

The Big Shift

The shifter is to be used only for shifting gears. It is not a place to rest your hand.

In shifting gears, your arm and hand motions must be smooth and precise. Slamming gears like a street racer is not the proper method, nor do you want to do anything that might throw off your car's balance.

The shift knob should be cupped firmly in your hand, not with a death grip. With practice, you will be able to shift smoothly and the revs won't kick up too high--which leads us to downshifting.

All braking and shifting should be executed while driving in a straight line. More advanced maneuvers will be taught by your instructors.

You downshift so that your car will be properly geared to accelerate away from a corner. Never try to slow the car with the clutch or by downshifting. That is what brakes are for. There is less material on the clutch disc than on the brake pads.

Instructors continually remind students, "You paid for the brake pads. Use them."

Downshifting must be practiced to achieve smoothness. If you are braking and shifting down, the right foot is usually on the brakes and left foot is on the clutch. That is fine, but when you take your foot off the clutch the rpms will shoot up, unsettle the car, and jerk the rear wheels. This action, in conjunction with braking, can cause the rear wheels to exceed their *traction* and skid.

There is a solution. When braking, keep the ball of your foot on the brake and slide the heel of your foot over to the gas pedal to boost the engine speed to the approximate rpm level needed to disengage the clutch. (This can be done three ways: by simply listening to the engine, by using a gear chart, or through experience with the car.)

DRIVING SCHOOLS

Because it is an advanced manuever, this heel and toe technique, or *downshifting while braking*, requires practice. But it provides a sense of control and safety.

Some cars have pedals so far apart that your heel could not reach even if you were double jointed. If that is your case, use the side of your foot or the other half of your foot.

Some cars may give you none of these options: you will have to complete all your braking and then slide your foot to the gas pedal. Be sure to discuss this with your instructor before your session, so he or she can work with you to make your downshifting as smooth and precise as possible.

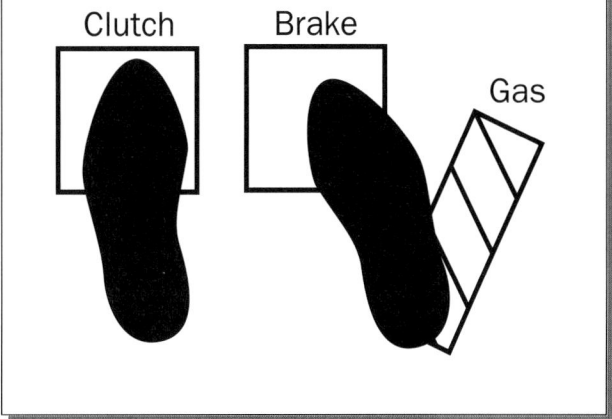

The heel and toe downshifting technique.

Cornering Maneuvers

The way you hold the steering wheel is an important part of control. The hands should always be at three and nine o'clock. Your fingers should wrap around the wheel with a firm grip, but never too tightly. If you jerk the wheel, you will unsettle the suspension and lose control. A death grip can actually cause jerkiness.

The only time your hands might move from three and nine would be upon entering a sharp corner. In this circumstance, I recommend a modified shuffle steer.

Many schools teach their own version of the shuffle steer, but I use this technique: in a left turn, slip your right hand down to the six o'clock position and push the wheel up to the three o'clock position. It is much easier to push the

DRIVING SCHOOLS

wheel than to pull it over. As you push the wheel upward, you can either let it slide through your left hand, or place your left hand at twelve o'clock.

After the turn, you would adjust your hand positions to unwind the wheel. This is the best way to get a good perspective on the corner.

Avoid crossing your arms when cornering for two reasons: steering corrections are impossible and your reach will be shortened.

When approaching any corner, concentrate on smoothness. Your initial turn-in should be fairly sharp and then smoothed out. Do not jerk the wheel. Never tilt your head, or your perspective of the corner will change.

When exiting a corner, you may need to unwind or readjust the wheel. Again, this should be done smoothly. Try to make as few adjustments as possible while driving through a corner.

Technique comes with practice. The difference between an average driver and an excellent driver is the manner in which they execute corners. Corners can come in many different forms, but all corners should be taken with the largest possible radius, to get the highest cornering speeds.

Think about a corner before you enter it. (Obviously you should know the course before you attempt it at full speed. Your instructors will insist on caution, but will gladly help you "see" the track from the beginning of your first session.) Setting up for a corner, think about the entry point, the gear you want for a proper exit, and the speed you want to carry through the corner.

Straight line hard braking and heel-and-toe downshifting should be completed at the exact time you reach the corner's entry point. Turn the steering wheel enough to point the car at the corner's apex and, once the wheel is in that

DRIVING SCHOOLS

position, try not to make any corrections. Look at the apex, with *eyes up*. Again, smoothness and precision are the goal.

If you turn the wheel too quickly or too far, you will either understeer or oversteer. If the rear wheels begin to slide, gently accelerate out. The weight transfer will make this work. As you approach the apex, begin to apply the gas so that you are at full throttle upon reaching the corner's exit. Then start to think about the next corner.

Andy Hillenburg of Fast Track High Performance Driving School gives pointers on maneuvering.

In order to have good lap times on a course, you must go as fast as you can for as long as you can. Obviously, because you must slow down to turn, corners do not contribute to your average speed. For that reason you want to extend your straights, and shorten your corners.

By braking as hard and as late as possible, you can still slow enough to enter a corner safely. If you maintain control through that corner, you are better positioned to fully accelerate at the apex and out of the corner. The sooner you are back up to speed, the better your average and lap time.

Most driving schools mark the entry, apex and exit points of a corner with pylons, so that you can distinguish them from a distance. This is a great help not just for beginners, but for everyone.

Balancing Act

It's impossible to over-emphasize the point that proper balance of the car is necessary for smoothness around the course.

Sudden movements, such as jumping on the brakes or gas, popping the clutch, jerking the

DRIVING SCHOOLS

steering wheel, or slam-shifting the transmission should never be a part of your driving technique on the track.

A turn into a corner should be progressive and smooth, without corrections and without *sawing* the wheel. If you are off-line, do not attempt to adjust the wheel. You might exit the corner too early, but this is okay because you will learn from these minor errors. Try to get it right next time.

Even with experience, you will still occasionally enter a corner too early or too late. Correct your mistake on the next lap. An instructor will always be with you to assist in perfecting your skills.

Finding The Ideal Apex

As mentioned earlier, taking a corner with the largest possible radius offers the highest possible cornering speeds.

That broad radius also means less braking is required before entering the corner. The key to that radius is the apex that is best both for the layout of the corner and for your car's ability to negotiate the corner.

A famous race driver once said, "I'd rather enter a corner slow and exit quickly, than enter the corner fast and come out dead." Keep this statement in the back of your mind.

There are several different types of apexes with which you will become familiar in time.

The theoretical apex is the point where the *largest possible radius* touches the inside middle of the corner. It can be found by bisecting the angle formed when you extend the edges of the corner (see corner diagrams).

The point you will use as your guide, however, is called the *practical apex* or *ideal line*, the best possible path through a corner considering all factors.

DRIVING SCHOOLS

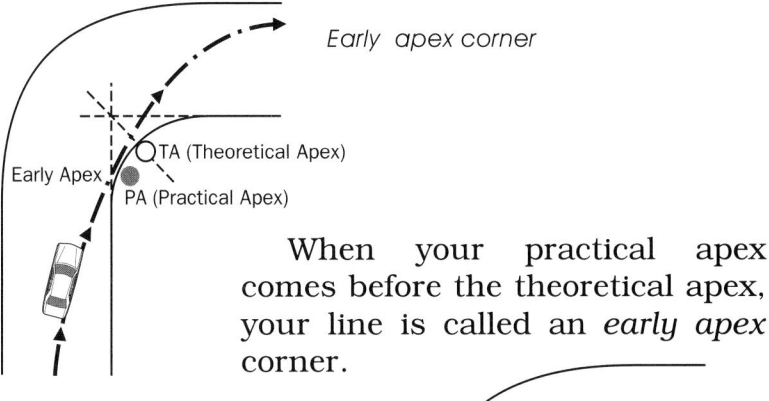

Early apex corner

When your practical apex comes before the theoretical apex, your line is called an *early apex* corner.

When your ideal apex falls after the theoretical apex, it is called a *late apex* corner.

Late apex corner

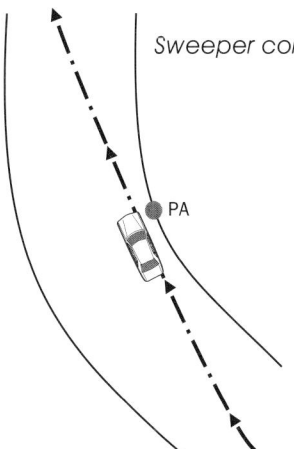

Sweeper corner

Sweepers are long corners that can be driven quickly, sometimes without braking. Whenever possible, try to use the whole road. Remember, eyes up throughout the corner is always best.

An *increasing radius corner* does not have a constant radius. It starts out tight, then opens to a wider turn at the exit. It is best to early apex this corner. You will be able to accelerate at a higher rate at the exit.

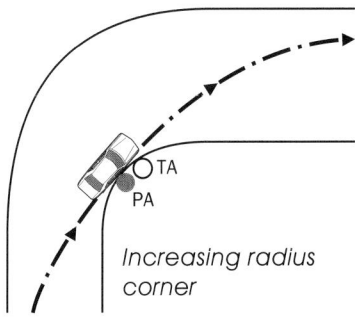

Increasing radius corner

DRIVING SCHOOLS

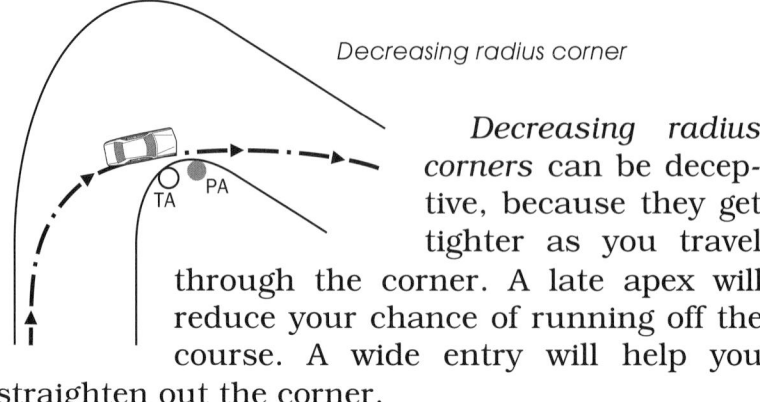

Decreasing radius corner

Decreasing radius corners can be deceptive, because they get tighter as you travel through the corner. A late apex will reduce your chance of running off the course. A wide entry will help you straighten out the corner.

Irregular corner

Irregular corners are a combination of two or more corners and do not fit any set layout. Some irregular corners may be treated as one corner, some as two. Each one must be analyzed with regard to your cornering, braking, and accelerating capabilities. Don't forget that your goal is a high average speed. Concentrate on the turn that gives the best exit when apexed. Don't let the rest of the track distract you.

Constant radius corner

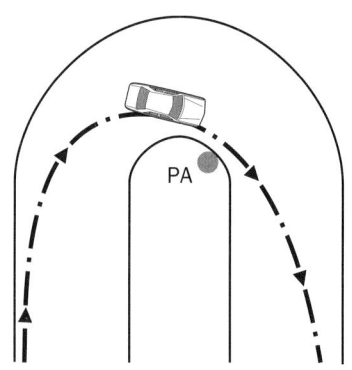

Approach a *constant radius corner* with a late apex. Go into it slowly so that you can take advantage of a higher exit speed.

DRIVING SCHOOLS

Carousel Corners are a combination of corners. Your approach should depend on how it is laid out. Sometimes carousels are long, sweeping corners and other times they are short corners. Choose the best line by dissecting the corner into two apexes. Make a slow sharp turn in the middle of the corner and straighten out for a high speed exit.

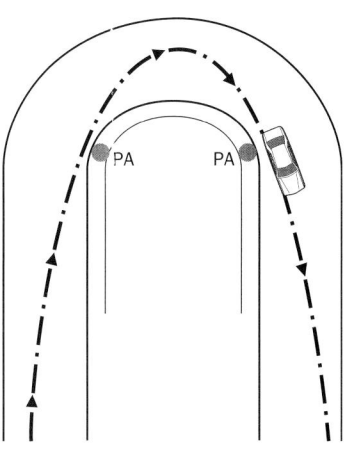

Carousel corner

Esses or compound corners are a combination of corners used to slow down your speed. They cannot be driven as one corner. Because of weight transfer, it is necessary to flatten out the corners as much as possible. That means a late apex corner.

Discuss the esses with your instructor, because each track has a slightly different design.

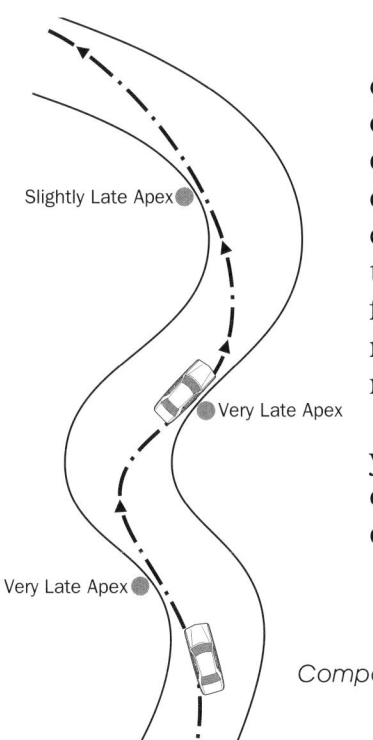

Compound corner

DRIVING SCHOOLS

Armchair Racing

Now that you have most of the details, let's put it all together and drive through a standard corner. Try to picture this in your mind, and practice whenever you can.

You will probably start on a straightaway, approaching the corner from the outside edge of the track. Your hands should be on the steering wheel at three and nine o'clock.

Think about that corner and how you will drive it. When you reach a braking point, squeeze on the brakes, using threshold braking, in a straight line. If you have to shift to a lower gear, use the heel and toe technique (downshifting while braking). Settle the suspension for the corner. Ideally, you should be at the apex just as you finish braking.

Do not coast to the apex. Constant *maintenance throttle* is best. When you reach the edge of the apex, start to apply power until you reach full acceleration. You should always progressively steer into the corner and hold the wheel firmly with both hands. Accelerate from the apex quickly or slowly, depending on the shape of the corner, as you unwind the steering wheel toward the exit. At the exit, do not be afraid to ride the edge of the track--this is called using the whole corner.

I cannot emphasize enough the need to be smooth while keeping your eyes up and looking ahead. With accuracy and lots of practice, cornering will become easy for you, and you will handle the basics of driving with ease.

After you have attended a few schools, you may want to look for other books to assist you in the direction of high speed events or high speed racing. This book is meant to give you the basics

DRIVING SCHOOLS

so that you can have your first taste before you arrive. This can help eliminate cold feet.

So, You Really Want To Race

There are many types of racing, and attending a drivers school is a great first step toward finding out what type is for you.

There are more types of high-speed racing than we can list in this book. Here are three samples to churn your brain and let you know about the possibilities. Start by talking with people in the type of racing that interests you most. If stock car racing is your dream, try that kind of school to learn what it is all about.

Solo I

Solo I, or hill climbs, is the easiest type of racing to get into. Contact the SCCA or your local hill climb chapter to find the right people. A Solo I event allows you to race at full speed on a race track, but there are safety and other regulations that must be followed, so get a copy of the rules.

Passing is not part of Solo I. There are three or four cars on the track at once, but they are carefully spaced to avoid the possibility of catching one another. Times are compared within classes, and the fastest time wins. This event can become quite competitive because it is based specifically on your driving abilities and your car's capabilities. Having a few driving schools under your belt definitely works in your favor.

Showroom Stock Racing

The SCCA runs regional and national races at every sanctioned track across the country almost year 'round. One of the more popular classes is showroom stock racing, which is based on the premise that you can purchase a brand new car, bolt in a roll cage and fire extinguisher, and go

DRIVING SCHOOLS

racing. You will need appropriate seatbelts and a few other safety items, but no modifications are allowed so you must choose your car wisely.

At the time of this writing, there are four showroom stock classes.

This sport can be expensive. Because your best chance to win is with the newest state-of-the-art technology, it could mean a new car every year. This type of racing can also be intensely competitive--a good way to establish a strong background before getting into more advanced racing classes.

Contact the SCCA for more information, general competition rules, and showroom stock rules and regulations.

Stock Car Racing

There are many different types of stock car racing. Locally, you may find entry level classes like Street Stock, Hobby Stock and Mini Stock. At the other end of the scale are the highly competitive series like the NASCAR Winston Cup circuit. For more detailed information on stock car racing in your area, inquire at your local stock car race track.

I had a fabulous time at the Fast Track School at Charlotte Motor Speedway in North Carolina. Participants got a bird's-eye view of the nuts and bolts of stock car racing. The school supplies its students with real NASCAR cars, instructors, helmets, and even drivers' suits. From the orientation session to the chassis session to the on-track sessions, the class is designed with one thing in mind: stock car racing. Students learn that watching stock car racing is much different than getting involved.

Participating offers an entirely different and more exciting perspective. Even if you don't plan

DRIVING SCHOOLS

Sunday Driving.

Somehow It's Different When You Belong To The Sports Car Club Of America

On Sundays SCCA members go road racing. At the local race circuit it's okay to exceed 55 mph. Or out-brake someone into turn one. The best news is SCCA offers safe participation in amateur and pro motorsports competition, be it road racing,  autocrossing or rallying. In  fact, we insist on it. There's lots of action across the country and plenty of ways to join in. Call toll-free for all the details: (800) 255-5550. Or write SCCA, 9033 E. Easter Place, Englewood, CO 80112. Put the fun back in your Sunday driving.

DRIVING SCHOOLS

on becoming a stock car racer, this is guaranteed to be the experience of a lifetime.

IT Racing

Showroom stock is great fun, but most of us cannot afford a new car every year. So *IT racing* was formed. The initials IT stand for "improved touring," and the format offers a great way to race inexpensively.

Participants must be SCCA members with a current SCCA club racing license. You can rent or borrow an IT car before you buy, but we suggest you contact your local SCCA regional group and speak with people already racing IT classes. Those folks can provide many helpful details to save you money, effort, and time.

IT race cars are generally too old to be legal for showroom stock classes. Of course, they can be updated for safety and performance. There are different IT classes based upon performance, and these competitive groups can provide plenty of fun. Contact your local regional group or the national headquarters of the SCCA for complete details and requirements.

Vintage Racing

Vintage racing is all about showing a historic race car in its natural environment, "at speed" on a road course. Vintage racers' goals are to have fun, at speed, and do it safely.

Many different marques are represented. It is not unusual to find Mini-Coopers, Shelby Mustangs, Cobras, Corvettes, Ferraris, and old Indy cars. Vintage racing is quickly becoming a popular high-speed racing activity.

Many of us are old enough to have raced in the '60s, and we remember when racing was much different. We can all relive those glory days by buying an old sanctioned race car and, with a few

DRIVING SCHOOLS

new restrictions, race against similar vehicles.

Vintage racing is quite competitive, but there is universal agreement that, while all of the drivers are out to win, no one wants an accident or even a close call. Many parts for the old race cars are hard to find, and each car has its own historic and dollar value. Therefore, competitors tend to be especially courteous, giving vintage racing a "gentleman's sport" reputation. If there is a fender-bender, the board of the sanctioning group often will review the circumstances to decide if one of the competitors is at fault.

Vintage racing stresses originality, with added safety aspects. Engines and bodywork must be stock, and no flared fenders or non-factory bolt-ons are allowed. Some of the safety updates allowed are carbon metallic brake pads, high-temperature brake fluids, and dual-chamber brake master cylinders. (Disc brakes are allowed only if they came that way from the factory. No updating or backdating is permitted.) Upgraded tires are allowed, but racing slicks are allowed only in certain classes. Roll bars are a must, as are updated fire extinguishers, fuel cells, five-point driver harnesses, window nets, and power shut-off switches.

While the largest of the Vintage racing organizations is the Sportscar Vintage Racing Association, or *SVRA*, there are dozens of vintage race groups running sanctioned events.

Individual vintage organizations will be able to assist you in more detail, so contact a local group to see if your car is among those eligible. Once you attend a vintage event, just to watch, you will get hooked.

Many people find that driving schools are enough to satisfy their need to race. Some will try

DRIVING SCHOOLS

to gain enough experience and ability to teach others to enjoy this type of auto fun. I hope this compels you to try many schools, and to continue to enjoy your car and learn more about driving.

I wish you the best in racing, if that is your future goal. Please remember that safety is something that you should never skimp on. It is the most important factor, from driving schools to the real action.

DRIVING SCHOOLS GLOSSARY

Italicized words found in this chapter:

Apex. A point along a curve where the largest possible radius touches the inside edge of the track.
Constant radius corner. Corner with a constant arc.
Corner workers. Your only source of information regarding track conditions while on course.
Decreasing radius corner. A corner that gets sharper and narrower.
Downshifting while braking. Also known as heel and toe. To downshift and brake at the same time, without upsetting the suspension.
Driving school. A fun and safe way to learn how to drive under controlled conditions.
Early apex. When the practical line is driven before the theoretical line.
Entry. The turn in point where one begins a corner.
Exit. The point of finishing a corner.
Eyes up. An expression used by many instructors to remind a driver to look as far ahead as possible, and to think ahead to the next corners.
Flags. The only communication you will receive about the rest of the track. Most events use standard flags.
Ideal line. The best possible path through a corner considering all factors.
Increasing radius corner. A corner that gets progressively wider.
IT racing. Improved touring racing. Contact the SCCA for more information.
Largest possible radius. The fastest line possible that still allows the car to still be on the track at the entry, apex, and exit.

Late apex. The safest way to drive the track. When the practical apex is before the theoretical apex.

Maintenance throttle. Not accelerating or decelerating; holding a constant throttle to maintain power.

Neutral steer. When a car does not understeer or oversteer; all four wheels maintain the same sliding characteristics.

Oversteer. When the car's rear tires feel as if they will break loose in a corner.

Practical apex. The ideal apex where the path of the car follows the inside edge of the track.

Sawing. Rapid back and forth movements of the wheel in order to correct your line through a corner. This is an incorrect procedure.

Solo I. Also called Hill Climbs. Contact the SCCA.

SVRA. A large vintage racing organization.

Traction. The ability of a tire to adhere to the track. This is a function of weight, tire compounds, and tire contact area.

Vintage racing. A fun way to put an older car with race history back on the track where it belongs. For more information, contact the SVRA.

CHAPTER 5

Car Shows
Details, Details

There is more to showing cars than just parking your nice car next to other nice cars. Details make any car. With show cars, they need to be the *correct* details.

Show cars range from the totally modified, to perfectly-detailed, 100 percent *concours*-restored. The direction you take is up to you and your tastes. I have had the best luck with concours restorations and mildly-modified cars, but this chapter contains many of the secrets to winning any of the varied classes.

I have been to shows where really nice cars have won their classes or *special awards*. I've also seen real pieces of junk win. It can be aggravating to lose under questionable circumstances, when even your competitors feel that you should have taken your class. Sometimes things are just not fair. Solid preparation is the only thing that can help you even the odds at shows.

People who go to car shows truly want to bring home a trophy, not just to spend a day in the rain or hot sun--and that's the bottom line.

CAR SHOWS

Sources

Before you initiate your detail work, shop around to get as much information as possible on available products. There are at least a dozen different interior parts manufacturers out there, all with different qualities and prices.

If you are looking for original parts, check out all avenues. There are con artists, as well as overpriced dealers. They figure you need it, they have it, and you will have to pay their price. Word of mouth is the best way to find the right supplies.

Now is the time to go to other people in your national club and ask for help. They will be happy to tell you who the legitimate vendors are, and will also give you some clues about which parts are still available from the dealer. I cannot over-emphasize the importance of joining the national club for your marque of vehicle.

The appendix lists names and addresses of major clubs that should be able to help you. Local regions may also be worth your time, but beware of local club problems. National clubs are your best bet, in addition to judges and friends with similar interests.

Preparation

It is always best to do your own preparation and detail work. Being a part of both the effort and success will make you appreciate your work, the expense, and your car even more. It sort of seems like cheating, or missing the point, to have someone else do all the work.

Once you have decided what to show, it is necessary to prepare your car appropriately. This means that you should be as consistent as possible.

CAR SHOWS

If you prefer modified cars, and you enjoy the chrome look, try to follow that same theme all the way through the car. For instance, a beautiful car that is all chromed and modified would look out of place with original tires and rims for that car. Consistency really makes the difference and will really help you come home with the trophies.

While there will always be someone who has the money to give their car and a blank check to a professional, you can do just as well on your own with time and patience.

If you prefer concours-correct cars, you will find the restoration can cost more than it first appears. I have learned over many years of restoration and judging experience that original cars must be extremely consistent to win. If a car is perfect in workmanship and originality, and a judge or spectator suddenly spots a non-factory air cleaner or radiator cap, the car's whole image deflates. Such items are sore-thumb obvious, and tend to greatly detract from the car.

Evening The Odds

How do you prepare a car to win? If you're starting from scratch, with an idea but no car, the first thing to do is choose a car that will stand out and catch attention. A crowd-pleaser is usually a winner. Choose a car that will appeal to the masses, like a musclecar, sports car, an exotic, or something really different. Stay away from family cars, daily driver-type cars, or everyday cars you see on the street.

Even experienced competitors go to car shows to see their dream cars--it may even seem at times that your obligation is to fulfill their dreams. So, make sure that the car you choose is one *you* like, one you want to work on, and also one you want to work with.

CAR SHOWS

How To Know How Far to Go

Everybody wants their car to be the best, a fact that has elevated car detailing to an art form of sorts. But undercoating the undercarriage or painting everything black to cover up details is not the best way to win.

If you are restoring a car, you will always run into a dilemma of whether to restore original paint or re-detail an original undercarriage. Seek the advice of experts and judges within that field.

For example, if you are restoring a 1965 Shelby, contact the Shelby American Automobile Club in Sharon, Connecticut; the 1965 Head Concours Judge; and the 1965 Shelby Registrar.

This "Best of Show" undercarriage shows how far concours competitors go.

The group that you contact will be more than happy to set you in the correct direction. A competitor may not tell you about correctly-detailed striped heater hoses or other details that may cause that person to gain more points in judging. Of course, there are many fabulous books available on restoration and car detailing for all kinds of cars.

To put it in perspective, visit a new car dealership and inspect a showroom model. Look under the car and under the hood, and take note of all the factory assembly inspection markings, all the labels and decals, the black paint, grays, body color, undercoating, and different colors of metal plating. Complicated?

A top-winning concours car should look just like it came off the showroom floor without the rustproofing. Don't *over-restore* your car. If a

CAR SHOWS

component did not come on the car from the factory, do not put it on. Unless you are building a modified car, do not vary from original parts and details. It may sound expensive to deal with all the additional details but, unless you hire a professional to do the work for you, you can accomplish a lot economically. All it takes is time, patience, personal commitment, and the will to complete your car correctly.

An original, concours-detailed engine compartment.

The Show For You

Now that your car is perfect in every way possible, it is time to look for the car shows in your area, or even a national show. The national organization for your marque of car will probably have a national convention somewhere in the country. Some people prepare their cars only for this event, so expect to see a different level of competition at this type of meet. Obviously, it is more prestigious to win at a national event than at a local show, and it won't hurt your car's resale value either.

You will need to have your car in top condition and be extra-prepared for a national show meet. The stress level can be high. Understandably, you'll feel you have the best car in the country, just like the guy parked next to you.

Do not be discouraged if you attend a national meet and do not win your first time out. It is even a good idea to attend the event the year before

CAR SHOWS

your car is completed so that you know what to expect. You may also find some new connections for parts. It really is nice to talk to people who love the same type of car you do. You'll almost feel like cousins, even with fellow competitors, and you'll meet some interesting people with fascinating stories and trade secrets.

If you want to start with local shows, attend a few cruise nights and keep your eyes open for flyers on the local schedules for your area. The only problem with local car shows is that their classes may be limited to categories like Musclecars (all), '70 to present Chevys, or Street Rods (all). This can make it difficult to win, especially if it is a popular vote show. It will also be difficult to get meaningful feedback from owners of cars like yours.

Some larger shows will break the classes down more specifically, and local regions of national clubs usually have one or more shows per year. For example, the Olds Club may break down years and models to similar body styles, sort of like a mini-national meet. When attending local shows you will probably hear about more upcoming shows, so leave your window down to receive flyers. It is common practice to distribute one-page announcements in this manner, so don't get upset if your front seat fills up with flyers about other shows.

Packing The Gear

If you trailer your car, be 99 percent prepared before you arrive. I spend several nights before the show making sure everything has been packed and considered.

If you drive your car to shows, as most people do, you will need to re-clean the car once you are

CAR SHOWS

in your spot for the day. Wash and wax the day before, clean the undercarriage, detail the engine compartment, wash the windows, and polish and shine your tires and rims.

The Packing List

Each time you show your car, bring along:

- **hand glaze** (try Imperial Hand Glaze), a good wax for touch-ups, a toothbrush to remove excess wax, and rags to apply and polish wax
- **chrome cleaner** (like Nevr-Dul or Metal Master)
- **tire polish** (Armorall or similar brand)
- **touch-up paint** in all the colors you use
- **cotton swabs** (Q-Tips) to clean those hard-to-reach areas
- **paper towels, newspaper, and glass cleaner**
- hand-held **vacuum cleaner** with a cigarette lighter adapter plug
- clean soft **rag or feather duster** to remove dust and road dirt
- **garbage bag** to clean your area at day's end

Keep a box of these items ready to go to speed your pre-show preparations. That box of goodies will help you clean your car properly, and keep it presentable throughout a show.

Fingerprints are bound to show up at any time, no matter how carefully you watch your car. (Some people let their kids touch anything.) Dust also tends to build up on darker cars, especially black cars.

Here's a little secret: Bring plain newspaper to the show to clean the window glass. With glass cleaner and newspaper instead of paper towels, you will actually polish the glass, with no streaking.

Keep the car as clean as possible until it is judged. For popular vote shows, you will have to clean the car periodically throughout the voting period.

CAR SHOWS

Additional Considerations

Besides cleaning supplies, bring something comfortable to sit on, preferably a foldable chair, an umbrella for sun and rain (most shows are held rain or shine unless a rain date is stated), a cooler stocked with food and drinks in case there are no concession stands, and anything else that will help you and your family enjoy the day. We also suggest that you bring your complete display to every show.

Unless you are bringing another car as a support vehicle, everything and everyone must fit into your car without damaging the interior or trunk. Don't overdo it--think of it as packing for a vacation. Everyone tends to overpack and then not use half of what they bring.

Judging And Competition

Arrival time is an important car show consideration. Your arrival time can make the difference between winning first place or going home empty-handed. If a show opens at 9:00 a.m., get there by at least 10:00 a.m. This will give you enough time to prepare your car and give it early exposure. It's a fact that *marketing* your car has an impact on judging. If you show up late, there may not be enough spaces available for you to park with your class. This is a sure way to be passed by and to end up with nothing.

The difference between the winners and everybody else may be determined by how the show is judged. The three most common forms of judging are *popular vote*, *cross judging* and concours judging. Popular vote judging is done by the people who are entrants and spectators.

Cross judging avoids the problems of open popular voting. Participants in "Class A" judge

CAR SHOWS

"Class B" by popular vote, and vice versa.

Popular and cross judging are both won by opinion and individual appeal.

Concours judging is more precise, and the most prestigious to win. Certified Concours judges are experts in their fields. Each club has its own standards. Ask for a copy of the judging form prior to a national meet for a better understanding of Concours standards.

Some people begin their popular voting prior to the commencement time announced by the event coordinators. This happens often--there is not much you can do about it except to be in place early. Sometimes a voter will not care about a specific class and will vote for the first car lined up in that class. This is another good reason to be there early and first in line for your class.

Bear in mind throughout the day that some spectators can be inconsiderate. Someone should remain with your car to watch for strollers, bikes, skateboards, and purses. Always ask in a polite manner that others take care. Everyone loves to have their car admired, so try not to be to harsh.

At a judged show, the first car there may be judged for a longer period of time than the other cars. In this case, we recommend that you line up second or third in your class. The reason for this is because judges figure they will hit every item on their judging form, until they realize it takes an hour or so. Only then do they realize that they must work faster and more efficiently.

This even happens with experienced judges. They speed up their inspections down the line and tend to be less picky. This is definitely to the advantage of the later cars to be judged. Nothing in this world is 100 percent perfect, so why give the judges a chance to pick your car apart? It will

CAR SHOWS

just drive you crazy.

You may notice that some judges will walk by all the cars first, and then judge in numerical order. Or they may spend more time with cars that catch their eyes and less time with others. You want to have a good first impression so that they will give you and your car a fair shot. This is another reason for displays and consistency.

Displays

Displays are an important part of winning a show, a type of product marketing.

Walk down a grocery store aisle and notice the position, place, and promotions for each product in a section. This will help you understand the need for a car show display of some sort. Walking down a row of beautiful cars, your eyes will almost always catch the car with the display.

The display must represent your car properly. Forget stuffed animals, toys, and assorted junk. You'll need something showing thought and character.

For example, Italian sports cars are associated with speed, Italy, and class. The display pictured here gives that Italian feeling, with a red and white checkered table cloth, grapes, cheese, Italian champagne, and a rose. To top it off, we play Italian classical music all day (hiding the radio for security).

The attention to the car itself is great, and the music makes it impossible to pass by without stopping for a

Sometimes it is best to have a display and the car stand out, but try not to go overboard.

CAR SHOWS

quick peek. This car and display have won many awards, including Best of Show.

Don't worry about hiring a professional to make you a display. Use your head and be creative. For concours shows that allow displays, we jack all four wheels off the ground about four inches with blocks of wood, and place mirrors underneath the car to show the undercarriage detailing. Mirrors provide a nice touch that allows people to enjoy your talents without bending over or getting their knees dirty on the ground.

A simple display of mirrors can enhance the details of any undercarriage.

Discount stores sell mirrors for a few dollars each. They're a good investment for showing cars.

Signs are another great way to attract attention to your car. However, a sign should not overpower the beauty of your car. It should be informative and relatively simple.

The more information you put down, the more people will shy away from reading it at all. Give basic information only. If someone wants to know more, they will definitely ask. So will the judges. This information is the most common :

- Name of car owner
- City and state
- Year, make, and model of car
- Serial or VIN if pertinent or rare
- Production figures, if limited
- Any factory rare model type information, or factory equipment that may be of interest
- Documented mileage (if low or unusual)

CAR SHOWS

- Anything unusual about the car's history (owners, factory, race car, etc.)
- If restored, when (month/year), and by whom

Optional information could include:

- Horsepower and torque ratings
- Drivetrain information, if unusual
- A special saying for your type of car. For example, "G.T. 350--Built To Be Driven," nothing dirty or silly.
- Winning achievements, such as national shows,

If you have the original window sticker or a copy of it, have all the information matted and framed. You might even add a sticker from any national club you belong to. It is always best to get that museum look, whether the car is stock or modified to the ultimate degree.

Propping the sign on an easel or a stand is also a nice touch. Place the sign at a distance from the car in case the wind catches it or someone bumps it down. Damaged paint from your own display will tear your heart out.

Your display also can include a pictorial of your restoration project from the original vehicle, through disassembly, paint, detail, and re-assembly to the beauty you have today. People who are really interested in your car may want to restore a similar one. This will give them clues to what is really involved. It will also show your qualifications as an expert on your type of car.

Factory literature is also a nice touch, and can be displayed in your trunk or on the dashboard. Keep an eye on this material if it has resale value.

Bringing trophies from previous events is your option, but only a few key ones are important. Too many will make you look like a showoff, and will only be a distraction. If the car has won that many trophies, its excellence will already be obvious to

CAR SHOWS

the spectators and judges.

A sign can be constructed from mirrors, Plexiglas, cardboard, posterboard, wood, and matted or framed pictures. I have even seen neon signs. The material is up to you, but remember to make it as clean and neat as possible. If you write it out freehand, it may distract from the car. Observe others at car shows to see what appeals to your tastes before you spend money or make your sign.

I have seen some unusual displays in my travels, from professionally-built booths (this is way overboard), to signs propped up against cars. All you really need is a detailed, clean, factory fresh-looking car with a clean, neat, and simple display to attract attention. Promote and market your car to win. Then you can go on to collect trophies and be proud of your workmanship.

A sign is essential, so add some creativity. But don't overcrowd it with information.

Show Day Comes To A Close

Once your car is judged, or the popular vote ballots have been collected, you are expected to leave your displays set up until trophy time. That's so that other owners and late-arriving spectators will not miss out on the overall pageantry of the car show. Also, if you must leave before the trophies are handed out, you could miss a special award, like "Best of Show."

If you absolutely have to leave early, inform the event coordinator of your circumstances and regrets. Handling it in that manner could mean that you will not be passed by for awards, and it will help you down the road at future shows.

CAR SHOWS

The bottom line is to show up early and stay until the end. Stay with your car during judging or popular voting, because everyone likes to ask questions.

CARS SHOWS GLOSSARY

Italicized words found in this chapter:

Concours. Restoring or detailing a car to its "new from the factory" condition, without additions, updating, or over-restoration. Concours shows are judged either on workmanship and originality or by popular vote.

Cross judging. A type of judging used at local car shows to avoid open popular voting. Class"A" judges class "B" by popular vote, and class "B" judges class "A" the same way. This can sometimes be unfair, so arrive at these types of shows early for good placement.

Displays. The best way to promote your car, including signs, mirrors, pictures and literature. Keep displays clean, simple, and neat.

Marketing. The three most important marketing points are its position at the show, its place in line, and its display. Without these, yours is just another car in a line.

Over-restore. To add to or change the way a car came from the factory. For example, a car that should have a red-oxide primer undercarriage would be over-restored with paint on the undercarriage body, or with too much plating where paint should be. This will cost an owner dearly at a concours event. Over-restoration does not apply to modified cars.

Popular vote. Voting process where either participants or spectators choose the cars they like best. This usually has nothing to do with whether a car is correct. Some people will vote for a friend's car, or all red cars, or none at all. An eye-catching display will always help at these types of shows.

Special award. An award given by event organizers or a select group of people for cars that excel in particular categories: Best of Show, Best Paint, Best Restoration, Best Interior, Best Chevy, etc.

CHAPTER 6

Before You Panic
No Substitute For Preparation

No matter how well you plan everything, from car shows to drag races to road races, things can go wrong. Sometimes, with either your car, the event, or your plans, Murphy's Law works too well.

How does it work? I have had my trailer loaded to go, only to find that an event had been canceled and we had not been notified. I have arrived at events that were filled to capacity, and the organizers couldn't find my entry. The list could go on, but one fact remains that none of us can control such things.

Frustration can be destructive to your enjoyment of the automotive sport and hobby. You need to learn to roll with it. After all your preliminary work is done, if that Great Race Chairman In The Sky says, "You are not racing or showing today," there's not much you can do.

On the other hand, there are numerous examples of situations that could have been prevented--which I'll try never to repeat. When a car is unfinished or unprepared, for instance, and has to be completed at the track or event, the nerve-racking stress does nothing for one's attitude. A perpetually bad mood will not help anyone win, have fun, or do well in general.

BEFORE YOU PANIC

Excuses (or reasons) are something we all give and hear when we do not win. Sometimes there are real reasons not to blame yourself, but try not to resort to clichés.

You will probably hear some of these from fellow competitors: "My run was slow because my clutch was not slipping properly," or, "My tachometer stopped working yesterday." A lack of understanding is the reason for many of these creative excuses.

The seasoned auto hobbyist will come to learn that almost anything can happen (or not happen). Planning and preparation is the best way to counter disappointment.

APPENDIX

Clubs and Organizations

This directory includes national organization and club names, with addresses and phone numbers where available.

If you do not find the club or organization that fits your need, check national magazines in the classifieds. Unless part of the formal name, organizations are not listed by the names of individuals associated with them.

Drag Racing

The Drag Racing School, Inc.
P.O. Box 140369
Gainesville, Florida 32614
(904) 373-7223
Gives personal instruction in prepared drag cars.

International Hot Rod Association (IHRA)
P.O. Box 3029
Bristol, TN 37625
615-764-1164
The $35/year membership includes *Drag Review*, *IHRA Rule Book*, patch, decal and hat pin.

APPENDIX

National Hot Rod Association (NHRA)
P.O. Box 5555
Glendora, CA 91740
Membership includes subscription to *National Dragster* and a copy of the *NHRA rule book*.

Road Rallying

Sports Car Club of America (SCCA)
9033 East Easter Place
P.O. Box 3278
Englewood, CO 80155-3278
(800) 255-5550
Membership includes a 1-year subscription to *Sportscar* magazine, a patch and a sticker. Rulebooks may be purchased seperately.

Autocross and Solo II

Sports Car Club of America (SCCA)
See previous listing.
Solo II rulebooks and Pro Solos information are available from your local region or from SCCA National Headquarters.

Driving Schools and Road Racing

Driving Schools

Bertil Roos Grand Prix Racing School
P.O. Box 221A
Blakeslee, PA 18610
(717) 646-7227

APPENDIX

**Bob Bondurant School
of High Performance Driving**
Phoenix, AZ
1-800-842-7223
The event is held at Firehawk Raceway, Arizona, with Ford Mustangs or Formula Ford race cars. The school offers instruction in Grand Prix racing, high performance driving, and advanced driving. Highway classes are also available.

**Fast Track
High Performance Driving School, Inc.**
P.O. Box 160
Harrisburg, NC 28075-0160
(704) 455-1700
The three-day Charlotte Motor Speedway event includes Winston Cup-style stock cars; driver's suit and regulation helmet are provided. An advanced oval course is also available.

Jim Russell Racing School
1023 Monterey-Salinas Highway
Salinas, CA 93908
(800) 821-8755 or (408) 372-7223
Race track: Laguna Seca Raceway
Courses also offered in Canada and England.

National Racing School
SCCA Enterprises
7476 S. Eagle St. #5
Englewood, CO 80231
(303) 693-2111

APPENDIX

The Skip Barber Racing School
Route 7
Canaan, CT 06018
(203) 824-0771 OR
29355 Arnold Drive
Sonoma, CA 95476
(707) 939-8000
This racing school includes Formula cars.

Track Time, Inc.
Performance Driving Schools
4600 Middle Drive, Suite A
Youngstown, OH 44505
(216) 759-1868
The event is available at many major race tracks, and includes both classroom instruction and one-on-one car instruction. Drive your own car or rent one of their cars.

Road Racing

SCCA
See previous listing
c/o Pro Division or Club Racing
SCCA offers about 10 classes to choose from.

Sportscar Vintage Racing Association (SVRA)
4 North Atlantic Wharf, Suite 201
Charleston, SC 29401
(803) 723-7872
c/o Frank Rupp

Vintage Auto Racing Association
3426 North Knoll Dr.
Los Angeles, CA 90068
(213) 874-9135
Attn.: Bettina Bennewitz

APPENDIX

Vintage Sports Car Club of America (VSCCA)
P.O. Box 1451
Chicago, IL 60690
(708) 534-7575
This club encourages the restoration and racing of vintage cars. Membership includes a monthly newsletter and a yearbook.

Car Clubs

For your local club, write to the national club.

International Show Car Association (ISCA)
32285 Mally Drive
Madison Heights, MI 48071
(313) 588-5568
Shows first-class, fully-detailed cars.

AMC
American Motors Owners Association
6565 Applegate Ln.
Louisville, KY 40228

AMX/Javelin Club of America
AMC performance cars
P.O. Box 9307
Daytona Beach, FL 32020

Chrysler
Mopar Muscle Club International
Rt. 9, Box 18
Lockport, IL 60441
(815) 838-8457

APPENDIX

National Hemi Owners Association
170 Pansy Pike
Blanchester, OH 45107

Ford

Cougar Club of America
18660 Rivercliff Park
Fairview Park, OH 44126
(216) 356-1291

Mustang Club of America (MCA)
P.O. Box 447
Lithonia, GA 30058
(404) 482-4822
Membership includes their monthly magazine.

Performance Ford Club of America (PFCA)
13155 U.S. Rt. 23
Ashville, OH 43103-0032
(614) 983-2273
Membership includes a bi-monthly magazine.

Shelby American Automobile Club
P.O. Box 788
Sharon, CT 06069
(203) 369-0449
Membership includes a bi-monthly newsletter and quarterly magazine (*Shelbys & Cobras*).

General Motors Cars

Buick

Buick Club of America
P.O. Box 898
Garden Grove, CA 92642

APPENDIX

Gran Sport Club of America
1213 Gromto Rd.
Valdosta, GA 31602

Cadillac

Cadillac Club International
P.O. Box 1
Palm Springs, CA 92263

Chevrolet

Camaro Owners of America
701 North Keyser Ave.
Scranton, PA 18508
(717) 346-7495

Classic Chevy Club International (1955-57)
P.O. Box 17188
Orlando, FL 32860
(305) 886-1957

Corvette Club of America
P.O. Box 30379
Washington, DC 20814

National Chevelle Owners Association
7343 West Friendly
Greensboro, NC 27410
(919) 854-8935

National Corvette Restorers Society
63370 CR19, Route 5
Goshen, IN 46526
(513) 385-8526 or (615) 938-1467

APPENDIX

National Council of Corvette Clubs, Inc.
P.O. Box 5032
Lafayette, IN 47903

National Monte Carlo Owners Associations
P.O. Box 187
Independence, KY 41051
(606) 491-2378

United States Camaro Club
1654 Mardon Dr.
Dayton, OH 45432
(513) 426-6494

Vintage Chevrolet Club of America
P.O. Box 5387
Orange, CA 92667

Oldsmobile

Hurst/Olds Club of America
1600 Knight Rd.
Ann Arbor, MI 48103-9303

National 4-4-2 Owners Club
P.O. Box 112014
Tacoma, WA 98411

Oldsmobile Club of America
P.O. Box 16216
Lansing, MI 48901

Pontiac

Fiero Owners Club of America
1941 East Edinger Ave.
Santa Ana, CA 92705
(714) 953-9400

APPENDIX

GTO Association of America Inc.
1634 Briarson Dr.
Saginaw, MI 48603

National Firebird Club
P.O. Box 11238
Chicago, IL 60611

Pontiac-Oakland Club International
P.O. Box 4789
Culver City, CA 90230

Trans-Am Club of America
P.O. Box 33085
North Royalton, OH 44133

Packard
Packards International Motor Car Club
302 French St.
Santa Ana, CA 92701
(714) 541-8431

Special Classes

Antique & Classic
Antique Automobile Club of America (AACA)
501 West Governor Rd.
Hershey, PA 17033
(717) 534-1910

Early Ford V-8 Club of America
P.O. Box 2122
San Leandro, CA 94577

Model A Restorers Club
24822 Michigan Ave.
Dearborn, MI 48124

APPENDIX

Foreign Cars

Austin-Healey Club of America
603 East Euclid
Arlington Heights, IL 60004
(312) 255-4069

BMW Car Club of America (BMWCCA)
345 Harvard St.
Cambridge, MA 02138
(617) 492-2500

DeTomaso Pantera Owners Club of America (POCA)
6417 Loma Ave.
Temple City, CA 91780

Ferrari Club of America
9632 Southeast City View Dr.
Portland, OR 97266
(503) 777-1240

Jaguar Clubs of North America
600 Willow Tree Rd.
Leonia, NJ 07605
(201) 592-5200

Mercedes-Benz Club of America
7467-250 Mission Gorge Rd.
Santee, CA 92071
(619) 448-0422

Porsche Club of America (PCA)
P.O. Box 10402
Alexandria, VA 22310
(703) 922-9300

APPENDIX

RX-7 Club of America
4020 Palos Verdes Dr., Suite 108
Rolling Hills, CA 90274
(213) 544-0822

Volkswagon Club of America
4419 Howard St.
Skokie, IL 60076
(312) 676-3787

Volvo Club of America
P.O. Box 710
Durham, NH 03824

Z Club of America (Datsun)
550 Lexington Ave.
Clifton, NJ 07011
(201) 546-9200

Muscle Cars

GM Musclecar Association
9 Vail Rd.
Landing, NJ 07850
(201) 770-0483

National Muscle Car Association
2095 Exeter Rd.
Germantown, TN 38138

National Street Rod Association
4030 Park Ave.
Memphis, TN 38111
(901) 452-4030

LOG BOOK

This log book is given as a guide for recording your events, the outcomes, and any changes made by you, the weather, or event officials. You may wish to customize your own book to better represent your level of competition or a specific activity.

Date	Event Type	Times or Placing

Tire Pressures	Changes Made	Other